ULTIMATE AIR FRYER COOKBOOK UK:

2000 Days of Healthy, Fast and Easy Recipes for Beginners to cook like a Pro

Alban Ray

Leave a review about our book:
As an independent author with a small marketing budget, reviews are my livelihood on this platform. If you enjoyed this book, I'd really appreciate it, if you left your honest feedback. You can do so by clicking review button.

I love hearing my readers and I personally read every single review!I

Table of Contents

AIR FRYER RECIPE BOOK

Are you tired of getting home after a long day just to get in the kitchen for an hour to work on a recipe for an hour with a mound of dishes in the sink? Are you fresh out of ideas on how to change up your dinner meal rotation? Are you tired of spending more time preparing a meal than enjoying it? We've got a solution for you. No one wants to get home from a busy day just to work more at the kitchen counter. An air fryer and our perfectly curated recipe book may be the answer for you.

What is this Book About?

Cooking the same things can become monotonous and a hassle, especially if you have a home full of picky eaters. We have created a collection of classic favourites and modern twists on meals that you just can't go wrong with - and it only takes one piece of equipment: an air fryer. This is your one-stop-shop guide for air fryer meals, fit for beginners and pros to learn healthier, faster ways to cook for your family with less cleanup. We know that you are busy, and we want to provide you with the ammunition that you need to crush it in the kitchen with delicious meals fast.

Who is this Book For?

The air fryer craze has revolutionised the culinary industry, enabling everyday people to cook restaurant-quality food with the click of a button. Whether you are a stay-at-home mom looking for easy ways to make a family-friendly meal while juggling kids all day or a beginner in the kitchen looking for a step-by-step guide on the ins and outs of your simple air fryer meals, this book is for you. We have especially crafted this air fryer recipe book for the busy bee that hardly has time to relax, let alone cook delicious meals. With restaurant-quality food available in minutes - you will never be tempted to order takeout again after a long day at the office or running around town.

What to Expect

The recipes in this book have been carefully curated to cater to you. With easy-to-prepare recipes that are healthy, quick to throw together, and British favourites, this book will quickly become your go-to when you're making a grocery list or scraping the bits and bots from your pantry together for a meal.

Don't expect to spend hours in your kitchen anymore. That was the old you. With this book in hand, you can start crafting the delicious meals of your dreams within minutes, freeing up your time to unwind after a busy day or enjoy a glass of wine on the sofa without a heap of dirty dishes to clean up after cooking a meal.

Who is Alban Ray?

Alban Ray has been figuring out the tools of the trade in the culinary industry for years now and has especially honed his craft of cooking with an air fryer. From throwing random ingredients from his cupboard together for a meal with friends to organising and planning professional-grade recipes, he's done it all. He, too, has struggled to find quick, healthy meals without the hassle or time commitment. You aren't alone, home chef! After learning about how to use and optimise the capacity of the air fryer, he is ready to share his experience with you. So, get ready, and get excited!

If you are looking to grow your understanding of how to cook with your fancy new kitchen gadget and are starting from square one, you have come to the right place. Alban has walked this road of discovering the best ways to maximise the life of your air fryer and is excited to share his experience. Get excited to get in your kitchen because the smells (and tastes) that will soon fill your home are going to be divine! The days of you spending hours in the kitchen slaving away over a meal are over. Welcome to your new favourite kitchen gadget and cookbook.

6

INTRODUCTION

Meals are a time of gathering. Of sharing laughs, or reliving memories, of delighting in culinary skills, and of experiencing togetherness. The one thing that can enhance the already wonderful times that happen around a table is a meal that blows your taste buds away. Now, it doesn't take just a culinary chef to make a culinary masterpiece. It is possible for the mundane homeowner or even university student in a cupboard-sized dormitory to make incredible dishes with one simple tool: an air fryer.

Introducing an air fryer to your kitchen gadget lineup is not something to be intimidated by or a useless tool to collect. Adding an air fryer to your arsenal is a practical way to condense multiple kitchen appliances into one gadget. Whether you need to saute, bake, steam, fry, or any other number of cooking methods, the air fryer has got your back, and without the icky mess to clean up afterwards.

This book is meant to help you, as the everyday home chef, feel empowered to get in the kitchen and get creative with this 150-recipe collection. The air fryer can be used from breakfast until dessert and every meal in between. You will likely reach for this book as you're crafting your grocery list and figuring out what to throw together for a last-minute family dinner.

Perfect for the busy home chef that doesn't have the time to make elaborate meals or research healthier alternatives to those oh-so-delicious greasy favourites, this book can provide easy and quick meals that are both healthy and delicious. Look no further than this book cover for your next weekly menu lineup.

How Does the Air Fryer Work?

The air fryer has become the latest fad in kitchen appliances and a must-have for every home chef. The countertop appliance promises restaurant-style foods without the cleanup, time commitment, hassle, or large pile of dishes in the sink that traditional cooking incurs. With minimum effort and a fraction of the oil that you would normally use, air frying is the new normal.

Air fryers are countertop cooking appliances that use a specialised heating element and internal fan to circulate hot air around your food, almost like a convection oven. The foods that you will have at dinner after cooking with your air fryer will be perfectly crispy on the outside and tenderly juicy on the inside without frying your foods in a massive pan of oil.

The air fryer has blown up in popularity over the past couple of years, making them widely available to any consumer. With small air fryers selling for less than 40 EUR to larger multi-functional models going for 300+ EUR, there is an appliance for every type of home chef. Most units have multiple cooking options, allowing users to choose from steaming, roasting, dehydrating, toasting, air frying, and baking settings. This could easily replace your large cabinet of kitchen appliances and make post-dinner cleanup exponentially more simple.

So, how does this technology work, anyway?

One of the beautiful things about air fryers that makes your meals healthier is that they don't actually fry anything. Instead, you simply place your food in a perforated basket, and the machine whirrs hot air around the food while it cooks. This convection effect creates the perfectly crispy and golden exterior of the food without over-cooking the tender inside of your favourite meals.

Cooking with an air fryer takes significantly less time and makes less of a mess than traditional deep frying. It also uses minimal oil, reducing the saturated fat and caloric content of your go-to meals at home. Air fryers typically have one of three cooking setups - a perforated basket, a wire rack, or a ceramic plate feature with holes in it to allow air circulation. This heat convection around the food cooks the outside of the food first, sealing in the moisture of your meal. The appliance will either have one or more cooking chambers, separating them into single-zone or dual-zone designations. The single-zone air fryer features a cooking basket, which can be large enough to cook an entire 1.5 kg chicken. Dual-zone air fryers have two chambers that enable users to cook two different foods at the same time with their own individualised settings.

It is important to note that you need to have ample space between items in the air fryer in order to ensure that each piece of chicken or individual brussel sprout has proper air circulation and isn't just crammed together on a single layer. Overcrowding your food could leave your meal soggy or unevenly cooked.

Benefits of Cooking with an Air Fryer

Of the many benefits of cooking with an air fryer, here are just a few:
- Healthier Meals
- All-in-One
- No Grease, No Mess
- Safer than Deep Frying
- Quick Meals for Busy People

Healthier Meals

One of the primary benefits of opting for an air fryer is that foods cooked in an air fryer are healthier compared to deep-fried foods that are drenched in cooking oil. According to many scientific studies, there has been a proven connection between eating a lot of fried foods and the risk of obesity. Deep-fried foods are high in fat and empty calories, leaving this alternative option to be one that is much healthier. The air fryer requires significantly less oil in order to create that perfect, golden crisp on your foods, compared to deep-fried foods. Some meals have up to 80% lower fat content than their deep-fried counterparts. This is huge for your diet journey and physical health. Switching over from deep-fried to air-fried meals can promote a healthier diet and ultimately help people shed pounds on their weight loss journeys.

However, air fryers only make your meals as healthy as the food that you put in them. Processed foods don't automatically become healthy because you use an air fryer to cook them. Be aware of the foods that you prepare and the amount of oil that you add, and you will be on your weight-loss or dieting journey in no time.

All-in-One

The air fryer has a cooking setting for everyone. From sauteeing to pressure cooking, steaming to air frying - the air fryer can replace many of your other cookware utensils and take up less space in your already-crowded kitchen cabinets. Some of the special functions of an air fryer help you get that restaurant-quality food without the smells, cleanup, and storage space demands of a commercial kitchen.

No Grease, No Mess

Because of the high-end technology that is involved in the air fryer, your food is essentially cooked with hot air. This means that cleanup is easy, grease-free, and less messy than the dreaded grease trap that is involved in cleaning up after frying in your kitchen. Say goodbye to scrubbing a nasty pan or "letting it soak" in the sink for a few days. Cleaning up your air fryer is as easy as 1-2-3.

Safer than Deep Frying

Deep frying foods incurs a risk of oil burns, which are not fun, to say the least. Using an air fryer is just as effective as deep frying without running the risk of splashing scalding hot oil on your skin or clothes.

Quick Meals for Busy People

Air fryers are also incredibly convenient, especially for working parents or busy people that want to eat home-cooked meals without spending hours in the kitchen each day. If you're one that has a tight schedule and doesn't have time to meal prep throughout the week, this really is a revolutionary tool for your kitchen. Common dinner components like chicken, potatoes, and veggies can be cooked in minutes. Switching to an air fryer will cut your time spent prepping, cooking, and cleaning your kitchen tremendously.

Cleaning and Maintaining Your Air Fryer

First and foremost, note that you should refrain from cooking anything that has wet batter, sauce, or any leafy greens. These don't do well in an air fryer and can become quite messy!

As with any home appliance, check out the owner's manual for more instructions and details on how to maintain and keep up with your new air fryer. As a general rule, we advise that you do a quick but thorough cleaning of your air fryer after each use. This will help prevent any buildup or unwanted grease or food particle spills, as well as prevent odour retention in your appliance. A periodic deep cleaning of your air fryer is also a great idea every once and a while to keep your air fryer in tip-top shape and in order to preserve the longevity of your appliance.

If you need an easy-to-clean option, look out for models that are dishwasher safe, and that have durable non-stick coatings. Do also consider what type of oil you are using, as aerosol-based oils sometimes have components that break down non-stick coating.

Before you start cleaning, make sure that the air fryer is unplugged and completely cooled down. If you are scrubbing any tough grease spots or stains, take care not to scratch the finish on the appliance.

After cleaning the air fryer, let it air dry completely before reassembling and placing it in your kitchen storage area. As with any electrical appliance, don't submerge the unit in the water!

20 Tips and Tricks to Get the Most Out of Your Air Fryer

The air fryer will absolutely revolutionise the way you use your kitchen space. Check out these tips to make sure that you are getting the most out of your air fryer's lifespan.

1. *Good Storage Spot.*
Find your air fryer a home in your kitchen that is even and heat-resistant. You also need to make sure that there is at least 10 cm between the wall and the air fryer exhaust vent.

2. *Pre-Heat Before Use.*
Preheating your air fryer is easy and effective. Simply set your target cooking temperature and let it sit for two or three minutes before placing the food in the air fryer basket. Once your timer goes off, your air fryer is ready to get cooking.

3. *Accessorise It.*
Once you get started air frying, it's hard to stop. You may even want to jazz up your dinner routine with some air fryer accessories. Oven-safe baking dishes or cake pans should be air-fryer-safe. The only tricky part may be whether or not the pans you already have on-hand fit into the air fryer basket or not.

4. *Invest in a Spray Bottle.*
Spraying oil is significantly easier (and fewer dishes) than drizzling or brushing and allows you to use less

oil when you're cooking. You can buy pre-canned oil sprays or simply add your oil of choice to an empty spray bottle.

5. *Use an Aluminum Foil Sling.*

Getting accessory pieces in and out of the air fryer basket can be a tricky task. You can use a folded piece of aluminium foil into a 5 cm x 50 cm strip to help. Place the cake pan, baking dish, or other cooking accessories on top of the foil strip. By holding the ends of the foil, you'll more easily be able to lift the pan and lower it into the basket. You can then tuck the ends of the foil into the basket and place the basket into the air fryer for cooking. When your timer has gone off, and it is time to return the pan, simply unfold and hold onto the ends of the foil to lift the pan out of the basket and voila!

6. *Develop a Proper Breading Technique.*

Many air-frying recipes call for home chefs to bread their meals before placing them in the basket. Breading is an important step. It is important to coat foods in this order: flour, egg, and breadcrumbs. Make sure that the breadcrumbs have stuck well to the food item; press them on well. Because air fryers are outfitted with a powerful fan for the air convection effect, you don't want loose breading to leave your chicken without crisp.

7. *Add Water to the Drawer when Cooking Fatty Foods.*

Adding water to the drawer underneath the basket in the air fryer can help prevent grease from getting too hot or smoking. This is especially helpful when cooking high-fat foods like bacon, hamburgers, or sausage.

8. *Don't Overcrowd the Basket.*

It is tempting to cook as much as possible at a time, but we cannot stress enough that overcrowding your basket will lead to soggy, unevenly-cooked food. You want beautifully golden, crispy food - so leave some wiggle room in your basket to allow for even air circulation during the cooking time!

9. *A Halfway Flip.*

Just as you would do if you were cooking on a skillet or on the grill, flip your food halfway through the cooking time for a more even finish with uniform browning.

10. *Open the Air Fryer Drawer to Check Doneness.*

One of the perks of using an air fryer is that you can open the drawer and check on the doneness of your food at any time throughout the cooking time. This will not interrupt the timing of your meal cooking, and the second that you replace the basket in the air fryer, the timer will start right where it stopped moments ago.

11. *Toothpicks.*

If you are cooking any lightweight ingredients with your meal in the air fryer, the fan that distributes air while cooking may blow it around. You can use toothpicks to fasten down, for example, the top slice of bread on your sandwich so that it doesn't blow around.

12. *Shake the Basket.*

Shaking the basket periodically throughout the cooking time can help redistribute the ingredients and cook more evenly.

13. *A Halfway Spray.*

If you prefer your foods to be a little extra crispy and golden, use a spray oil halfway through the cooking time to help your food brown more evenly.

14. *R emove the Basket Before Dumping Out Foods.*

The drawer below the perforated basket catches a lot of the juices, oils, and/or marinades that drop off of your meal. You need to ensure that you have unlocked and removed the basket drawer completely before turning out the food. Otherwise, you will have a greasy, juicy mess on your plate.

15. *Clean the Appliance Well.*

It is imperative that you at least rinse the basket and drawer after each use. These pieces are so easy to clean, so there is no excuse for being lazy here. This will help extend the longevity of your air fryer and reduce the risk of food contamination between meals.

16. Use the Air Fryer Settings to Dry Itself.

After washing the air fryer interior basket and drawer, you can pop them back into the air fryer and turn them on for two to three minutes. This will dry out the washed components better than hand-drying them with a towel would.

17. Reheating.

You don't have to only use your air fryer for cooking your meal. Use it to reheat your next-day leftovers too! Microwaves can leave your food soggy, and ovens can dry your leftovers out. Using an air fryer can match that fresh food texture within minutes.

18. Watch for Smoke.

If you notice either white or black smoke coming from your air fryer, it is an indicator that you may need to intervene. White smoke is an indicator that you may need to add some water to the air fryer basket. The grease has likely drained into the drawer and is burning, and water can help prevent this. Black smoke indicates that you need to turn off the air fryer immediately and look at the heating element inside the fryer. Food may have popped and attached to the heating element and started burning.

19. Easy-Clean Liner.

Adding a layer of parchment paper is a quick and easy way to make cleaning up the bottom drawer of your air fryer more simple and less messy. This is especially helpful if you are cooking anything that has been marinated.

20. Thermometer.

If you are making a roast, chicken, or any other type of meat that is in a big piece, we advise that you invest in a good meat thermometer so that you don't have to slice into each piece of meat to check its doneness. This is a necessity when cooking burgers and steaks, especially when people have personal preferences regarding their meat doneness or colour.

A Grocery List for Your Favorite Air Fryer Recipes

We have drafted an easy grocery list for you that contains a vast majority of the ingredients you will need to make the 150 recipes that are encapsulated in the following pages. Bring this book along with you on your next grocery run, and you won't have to make those annoying mid-week trips to restock your grocery essentials.

Produce - Fruits and Vegetables

- Potatoes
- Tenderstem Broccoli
- Green Beans
- Green Peas
- Onion
- Garlic
- Broccolini
- Cabbage
- Tomatoes
- Swede/Rutabaga
- Carrots

Dairy

- Shredded Cheese
  (mozzarella, gouda, parmesan, cheddar)
- Eggs
- Butter
- Milk
- Suet
- Natural Yoghourt
- Buttermilk
- Extra-firm Tofu
- Halloumi
- Heavy Cream
- Ice Cream

Baked Goods

- Frozen Puff Pastry
- Shortcrust Pastry
- Dumpling Wrappers
- Crumpets
- English Muffins
- Pie Crust
- Pizza Dough
- Pitas
- Corn Tortillas
- Naan

Oils, Vinegar, and Condiments

- Olive Oil
- Grapeseed Oil
- BBQ Sauce
- Piri Marinade Sauce
- Dijon Mustard
- Lemon Juice
- Strawberry Jam
- Hot Sauce

- Vegetable Oil
- Tomato Ketchup
- Rice Wine Vinegar
- Soy Sauce
- Sweet Chilli Sauce
- Mustard
- Mayonnaise
- Teriyaki Sauce

Seafood

- Cod fillets
- Kippers
- Crab Meat
- Shrimp
- Tuna Steaks
- Haddock fillets
- Scallops
- Salmon
- Striped Bass

Seafood

- Cod fillets
- Kippers
- Crab Meat
- Shrimp
- Tuna Steaks
- Haddock fillets
- Scallops
- Salmon
- Striped Bass

Meat

- Bacon
- Ground Beef
- Beef Eye Fillet
- Prosciutto
- Haggis
- Sausages
- Chipolatas
- Rump Steaks
- Mini Pepperonis
- Pork Tenderloin

Poultry

- Chicken Thighs
- Chicken Drumsticks
- Whole Chicken
- Chicken Breasts
- Ground Chicken
- Turkey Crown
- Turkey Breast

Seasonings

- Paprika
- Chips Seasoning
- Curry Powder
- Salt
- Pepper
- Garlic
- Piri Piri Seasoning
- Fajita Seasoning
- Cumin
- Cayenne
- Chili Powder
- Nando's Peri Peri Hot Rub

Dry Goods

- Breadcrumbs
- Instant Mashed Potatoes
- Plain Flour
- Cornflour
- Chicken Stock
- Vegetable Stock
- Beef Stock
- Dijon Mustard
- Vanilla Extract
- Self-Raising Flour
- Baking Powder
- Caster Sugar
- Raisins
- Oatmeal
- Wholemeal Flour
- Salt
- Bicarbonate of Soda
- Honey
- Icing Sugar
- Brown Sugar
- Sunflower Oil
- Granulated Sugar
- Cocoa Powder
- Worcestershire Sauce
- Pumpkin Puree
- Raisins
- Dried Apricots
- Oreos
- Oats
- Pancake Mix
- Peanut Butter

Herbs

- Rosemary
- Parsley
- Thyme

This page is for your notes

CHAPTER 1

BREAKFAST RECIPES

Air Fryer Sausages

Prep Time: 5 minutes
Cooking Time: 12 minutes
Total Time: 17 minutes
Servings: 6
Difficulty: Easy

INGREDIENTS

- 6 sausages
- 3 sprays of oil

DIRECTIONS

1. Preheat the air fryer to a temperature of 180 °C/360 °F for 5-ish minutes.
2. Prick each sausage a few times with a sharp knife in random spots.
3. Spray the base of the air fryer basket with a few squirts of oil. This will help prevent the sausages from sticking to the basket.
4. Use a pair of kitchen tongs to carefully place the sausages in the air fryer basket.
5. Set a timer for 12 minutes, adjusting the time accordingly based on the size of the sausages and if they are frozen or not.
6. Halfway through the cooking time, flip the sausages over with a pair of tongs to promote even cooking.
7. After the 12-minute timer, check your sausages and cook for longer if needed.

Nutrition Information

Calories 209, Fat 17 g, Saturates 6 g,
Protein 11 g, Carbs 2 g

Air Fryer Muffins

Prep Time: 10 minutes
Cooking Time: 15 minutes
Total Time: 25 minutes
Servings: 6-8
Difficulty: Not too tricky

INGREDIENTS

- 150 g self-raising flour
- 100 g golden caster sugar
- 75 g natural yoghourt
- 75 g blueberries, chocolate chips or dried fruit
- 2 tbsp milk
- 60 mL vegetable oil
- 1 egg
- ¼ tsp bicarbonate of soda

DIRECTIONS

1. Heat the air fryer to 160 °C/320 °F for 2 minutes. Mix the oil, yoghurt, milk, and egg in a large bowl until a smooth consistency. Fold in the sugar, flour, and bicarbonate of soda, combining well.
2. Fold in your blueberries (or chocolate chips or dried fruit), then spoon the muffin batter into silicone cases or an air fryer muffin tin accessory. Only fill the tins ¾ of the way full. You may have to bake your muffins in batches.
3. Place the cases/tins in the air fryer basket and cook for 12-15 minutes until the muffins are golden brown and the centre of each muffin is cooked through.

Nutrition Information

Calories 208,9 g, Fat 1 g, Saturates 14 g,
Sugar 0 g, Sodium 3 g, Protein 3 g,
Carbs 28 g, Fibre 1 g

Air Fryer Flapjacks

Prep Time: 3 minutes
Cooking Time: 15 minutes
Total Time: 18 minutes
Servings: 4
Difficulty: Not too tricky

INGREDIENTS

- 250 g gluten-free oats
- 100 g butter
- 100 g brown sugar
- 2 tbsp honey

DIRECTIONS

1. Place the air fryer grill pan inside the air fryer. Add the baking pan on top of it so that it slots into place.
2. Dice the butter into quarters and add it to the baking pan.
3. Cook the butter for 2 minutes at a temperature of 180 °C/360 °F until the butter is melted.
4. Blend the gluten-free oats in the blender until a breadcrumb consistency is achieved. Add the honey and brown sugar, then stir together well.
5. Cook the flapjacks for 10 minutes at 160 °C/320 °F, then for an additional 5 minutes at 180 °C/360 °F.

Nutrition Information

Calories 543, Fat 24 g, Saturates 13 g, Sugar 33 g, Sodium 189 mg, Protein 8 g, Carbs 75 g, Fibre 6 g

Cheesy Kale Nests

Prep Time: 20 minutes
Cooking Time: 20 minutes
Total Time: 40 minutes
Servings: 24
Difficulty: Not too tricky

INGREDIENTS

- 227 g Tuscan kale, stemmed, leaves halved lengthwise, then sliced thinly crosswise
- 1 tsp olive oil
- Kosher salt, to taste
- Pepper, to taste
- 2 large eggs
- 1 scallion, finely chopped
- 2 cloves garlic, grated
- ½ c almond flour
- 1 ½ tbsp all-purpose flour
- ½ tsp baking powder
- 4 oz shredded extra-sharp white cheddar cheese

DIRECTIONS

1. Heat the air fryer to 200 °C/400 °F.
2. In a large bowl, coat the kale with ½ tsp salt and olive oil. Transfer the kale to the air fryer basket and cook until wilted, approximately 1 minute. Return the kale to the same large bowl and let it cool.
3. Whisk together the eggs, scallion, and garlic in a large bowl and the baking powder and both flours in a smaller bowl. Fold the egg mixture, flour mixture, and cheese into the kale.
4. Line the air fryer basket with a piece of parchment paper, leaving enough room around the edges for good air circulation. You will most likely need to work in batches. Place 1 tbsp full of the egg nest mixture into the basket, spacing the nests about 2 cm apart.
5. Cook the nests until they are golden-coloured, about 4 minutes. After 4 minutes, flip each nest and cook one minute more until the edges are crisp and the nest is golden.

Nutrition Information

Calories 46, Fat 4 g, Saturates 2 g, Sodium 95 mg, Protein 3 g, Carbs 2 g Fibre 1 g

Air Fryer Breakfast Sandwiches

Prep Time: 5 minutes
Cooking Time: 20 minutes
Total Time: 25 minutes
Servings: 1
Difficulty: Not too tricky

INGREDIENTS

- 1 English muffin divided
- 1 large egg
- 2 slices bacon, cooked

DIRECTIONS

1. We Grease a ramekin with cooking spray, then crack your egg inside of it.
2. Place the English muffin and egg inside the air fryer basket. Set the temperature to 165 °C/330 °F and cook for 3 minutes.
3. Remove the English muffin from the air fryer and place the bacon in. Continue cooking the egg and bacon for 2 more minutes. Remove the egg, then turn up the air fryer temperature to 200 °C/400 °F and cook the bacon for an additional 3 minutes.
4. Place one half of the English muffin down on the cutting board, flip the egg on top, and top with bacon, followed by the second half of the muffin.

Nutrition Information

Calories 223, Fat 8 g, Saturates 3 g, Sugar 0 g, Sodium 338 mg, Protein 11 g, Carbs 72 g, Fibre 2 g

Air Fryer English Muffin Breakfast Pizzas

Prep Time: 5 minutes
Cooking Time: 10 minutes
Total Time: 15 minutes
Servings: 2
Difficulty: Not too tricky

INGREDIENTS

- 1 English muffin
- ¼ c pizza sauce
- 2 eggs
- 1/2c shredded mozzarella cheese
- ¼ c mini pepperoni

DIRECTIONS

1. Slice the English muffin in ½ and scoop out the centre of the bread for a little cavity.
2. Top each half of the muffin with 2 tbsp pizza sauce.
3. Crack an egg over the centre of the muffin and top with a pinch of salt and pepper.
4. Top the egg with shredded cheese, followed by mini pepperonis.
5. Place the pizzas in your air fryer basket and cook at 190 °C/380 °F for 8-10 minutes or until you notice that the egg whites are set.

Nutrition Information

Calories 329, Fat 19 g, Saturates 8 g, Sugar 2, Sodium 779 mg, Protein 19 g, Carbs 21g, Fibre 3 g

Air Fryer Breakfast Bombs

Prep Time: 5 minutes
Cooking Time: 15 minutes
Total Time: 20 minutes
Servings: 4
Difficulty: Show off

INGREDIENTS

- Olive oil cooking spray
- 3 large eggs
- 2 tsp whole milk
- ¼ tsp salt
- ¼ c cooked black beans
- ¼ c pico de gallo
- ½ c shredded pepper jack cheese
- All-purpose flour
- 227 g pizza dough

DIRECTIONS

1. Grease a 15 cm circular cake pan with cooking spray.
2. Whisk the eggs, milk and salt in a bowl together. Stir in the beans and pico de gallo.
3. Pour the egg mixture into the cake pan, then place the pan in the air fryer basket at 150 °C/300 °F for 8-10 minutes. Stir and scrape the sides of the pan every 2 minutes or so until the eggs are scrambled and cooked through.
4. Divide the dough on a lightly floured work surface into 4 pieces. Roll each piece into 13 cm round discs. Divide the egg mixture between each of the rounds. Bring the edges of the dough together, pinching the dough together to seal it. Spray each dough ball with cooking spray.
5. Spray the air fryer basket with a thin layer of cooking spray, then place the breakfast bombs into the basket, arranged in a single layer. Cook the dough balls at 175 °C/350 °F for 10 minutes or until the dough is golden and crispy.

Nutrition Information

Calories 276, Fat 21 g, Saturates 7 g, Sugar 1 g, Sodium 575 mg, Protein 15 g, Carbs 6 g, Fibre 0 g

Air Fried French Toast Sticks

Prep Time: 10 minutes
Cooking Time: 10 minutes
Total Time: 20 minutes
Servings: 6
Difficulty: Not too tricky

INGREDIENTS

- 4 eggs
- ½ c milk
- ¼ tsp vanilla extract
- ¼ tsp ground cinnamon
- 1/3 c granulated sugar
- 6 slices white bread, cut into thirds
- Cooking spray
- Maple syrup for serving

DIRECTIONS

1. Whisk the eggs, milk, vanilla extract, cinnamon, and sugar together in a small bowl.
2. Coat the air fryer basket with cooking spray.
3. Dip each piece of bread into the egg mixture solution and let the excess drip off, then place it in the air fryer basket.
4. Set the temperature to 200 °C/400 °F, then set the timer to 10 minutes. Halfway through, flip the bread sticks over to ensure even cooking.
5. When done cooking, drizzle with maple syrup.

Nutrition Information

Calories 374, Fat 10 g, Saturates 3 g, Sugar 4 g, Sodium 463 mg, Protein 15 g, Carbs 53 g, Fibre 3 g

Air Fryer Breakfast Bowl

Prep Time: 5 minutes
Cooking Time: 16 minutes
Total Time: 21 minutes
Servings: 2
Difficulty: Easy

INGREDIENTS

- 5 chicken nuggets, frozen
- 10 tater tots, frozen
- 4 eggs scrambled
- ¼ c milk
- ¼ c shredded cheese

DIRECTIONS

1. Preheat the air fryer to a temperature of 200 °C/400 °F.
2. Add the chicken nuggets and the tater tots to the air fryer basket, then cook for 6 minutes.
3. While the nuggets and tots are in the air fryer, add the eggs and milk to a small bowl and mix until combined.
4. Chop the chicken and tots into small, bite-sized pieces once done cooking.
5. Pour the egg mixture into an 18 cm pan, then top with the chicken nuggets and potatoes.
6. Decrease the air fryer temperature to 175 °C/350 °F, then cook the contents of the small baking pan for 7 minutes. Scramble the eggs and mix things up with a fork, then return the tin to the air fryer for 3 more minutes.
7. Top the breakfast bowl with cheese, then return to the air fryer for 1 additional minute.

Nutrition Information

Calories 549, Fat 37 g, Saturates 12 g,
Sugar 2 g, Sodium 508 mg, Protein 0,5 g,
Carbs 14 g, Fibre 1 g

Air Fryer Egg in a Basket

Prep Time: 1 minute
Cooking Time: 9 minutes
Total Time: 10 minutes
Servings: 1
Difficulty: Easy

INGREDIENTS

- 1 slice bread
- 1 egg

DIRECTIONS

1. Preheat the air fryer to 165 °C/330 °F, then spray the basket with nonstick cooking spray and add a piece of parchment paper.
2. Use a large cookie cutter to cut a hole in the centre of the piece of bread. Place the slice of bread on the parchment paper in the basket, then crack an egg into the centre of the bread.
3. Cook the egg in a basket for 5 minutes, then flip for an additional 3-4 minutes.

Nutrition Information

Calories 139, Fat 5 g, Saturates 2 g,
Sugar 2 g, Sodium 208 mg, Protein 8 g,
Carbs 14 g, Fibre 1 g

This page is for your notes

This page is for your notes

CHAPTER 2

FISH AND SEAFOOD RECIPES

Air Fryer Breaded Fish Fillets

Prep Time: 5 minutes
Cooking Time: 20 minutes
Total Time: 25 minutes
Servings: 1
Difficulty: Show off

INGREDIENTS

- 100 g cod fillets
- 40 g breadcrumbs
- 1 large egg, beaten
- 2 tbsp plain flour
- 1 tbsp parmesan cheese
- 1 tsp dried basil
- Salt and pepper, to taste

DIRECTIONS

1. Add the flour to a bowl and coat the cod fillets in the flour.
2. In a separate bowl, mix the breadcrumbs, parmesan, dried basil, salt, and pepper together until well-combined.
3. Dip the fillets in a bowl with the beaten egg, followed by the bowl with the seasoned breadcrumbs.
4. Spray the fish fillets with oil, coating all sides of the fish, and place them in the air fryer at 190 °C/380 °F for 15-20 minutes or until golden brown. Flip the fish over at approximately the halfway mark to ensure even cooking and browning on the fish.

Nutrition Information

Calories 303, Fat 8 g, Saturates 3 g,
Sugar 1 g, Sodium 689 mg, Protein 32g,
Carbs 24 g, Fibre 1 g

Chilli and Garlic Glazed Kippers

Prep Time: 5 minutes
Cooking Time: 10 minutes
Total Time: 15 minutes
Servings: 8
Difficulty: Not too tricky

INGREDIENTS

- 2 x 100g kippers
- 1 tsp salt
- 1 tsp pepper
- 1 tsp chilli powder
- 1 tsp paprika
- 1 tsp Italian seasoning
- 1 tsp garlic powder

DIRECTIONS

1. Season the Kippers. Add the chilli powder, garlic powder, paprika, salt, pepper, and Italian seasoning in a bowl. Mix the seasonings until well incorporated, then rub the seasoning onto the kippers.
2. Set the air fryer temperature to 200 °C/400 °F. Spray the air fryer basket with a thin layer of oil, then add the kippers, skin-side down, into the air fryer basket. Cook for 10 minutes and check to make sure that it is cooked to your liking.

Nutrition Information

Calories 7, Fat 12 g, Saturates 3 g,
Sugar 0g, Sodium 918 mg, Protein 25 g,
Carbs 0 g, Fibre 0 g

Air Fryer Fish and Chips

Prep Time: 5 minutes
Cooking Time: 10 minutes
Total Time: 15 minutes
Servings: 4
Difficulty: Not too tricky

INGREDIENTS

- ½ cup all-purpose flour
- 2 tsp paprika
- ½ tsp garlic powder
- ½ tsp salt
- ¼ tsp black pepper
- 1 large egg, beaten
- ½ cup breadcrumbs
- 2 kg cod fillet, cut into strips
- Cooking oil/spray
- Tartar sauce
- Lemon wedges

DIRECTIONS

1. In a small bowl, mix the flour, paprika, garlic powder, salt, and black pepper. Place the beaten egg in a second bowl and the breadcrumbs in a third bowl.
2. Pat the surface of the fish dry with a paper towel, then dredge the fish fillet in the flour mixture, followed by the beaten egg and breadcrumbs. Press the breadcrumbs onto the fish firmly, ensuring that they stick. Spray both sides of the fish with oil.
3. Set your air fryer timer to 200 °C/400 °F, and place the fish fillets in the air fryer basket. Cook them for 10-12 minutes, flipping them over halfway through the cooking time. You want the fish to be perfectly light and golden.
4. Serve with lemon wedges and tartar sauce.

Nutrition Information

Calories 220, Fat 2 g, Saturates 1 g, Sugar 1 g, Sodium 424 g, Protein 24 g, Carbs 18 g, Fibre 1 g

Air Fryer Salmon

Prep Time: 5 minutes
Cooking Time: 10 minutes
Total Time: 15 minutes
Servings: 4
Difficulty: Not too tricky

INGREDIENTS

- 4 salmon fillets, skin on or removed
- 1 tsp salt
- 1 tsp pepper
- 1 tsp mixed herbs
- 1 tsp garlic powder
- ½ tbsp olive oil

DIRECTIONS

1. Combine the salt, pepper, mixed herbs, and garlic powder in a bowl, and spread the seasoning mix onto a plate. Rub the dry seasoning mix onto each salmon fillet with a little bit of olive oil.
2. Place the salmon fillets in the air fryer basket in a single layer, being mindful not to overcrowd them. Cook the fillets in the air fryer for 8-10 minutes, set at a temperature of 180 °C/360 °F. Larger salmon fillets may need to be cooked longer, so if they are not cooked to your preference after the allotted time, continue cooking in 1–2-minute stretches.

Nutrition Information

Calories 264, Fat 17 g, Saturates 3 g, Sugar 0 g, Sodium 1 g, Protein 27 g, Carbs 0 g, Fibre 0 g

Air Fryer Scampi and Chips

Prep Time: 0 minutes
Cooking Time: 20 minutes
Total Time: 20 minutes
Servings: 4
Difficulty: Easy

INGREDIENTS

- 1 pack of frozen scampi
- ½ bag of frozen chips

DIRECTIONS

1. Remove the frozen chips from the bag and add them to ½ of the basket of the air fryer. Air fry for 5 minutes at 180 °C/360 °F.
2. When the air fryer beeps, shale the chips, then add the frozen scampi to the other half of the air fryer basket. Air fry the chips and scampi for an additional 8 minutes at the same temperature.
3. Spray the perimeter of the air fryer basket with oil and shake the chips and scampi, then air fry for 7 more minutes at 200 °C/400 °F.

Nutrition Information

Calories 1005, Fat 16 g, Saturates 2 g, Sugar 1 g, Protein 11 g, Carbs 54 g, Fibre 5 g

---

Striped Bass with Radish Salsa Verde

Prep Time: 10 minutes
Cooking Time: 10 minutes
Total Time: 20 minutes
Servings: 4
Difficulty: Show off

INGREDIENTS

- 1 garlic clove, crushed
- 1 tbsp anchovy paste or 3 anchovies, finely chopped
- ½ small red onion, finely chopped
- 1 tbsp red wine vinegar
- ½ c+ 1 tbsp olive oil. Divided
- 1 bunch radishes, diced, and leaves separated and finely chopped
- 1 c flat-leaf parsley, finely chopped
- 1 tsp tarragon leaves, finely chopped
- 4 6-oz fillets of striped bass
- Kosher salt, to taste
- Pepper, to taste

DIRECTIONS

1. Combine the garlic, anchovy paste, onion, and vinegar in a medium bowl and let it sit for 5 minutes.
2. Add the ½ cup oil, radishes, greens, parsley, and tarragon, and mix.
3. Heat the air fryer to 200 °C/400 °F.
4. Pat the fish dry and season it with ½ tsp salt and pepper each. Cook the fish skin-side down for about 8-10 minutes, or until the skin looks crispy and brown and the fish is opaque.
5. Serve with the radish salsa verde.

Nutrition Information

Calories 465, Fat 36 g, Saturates 5 g, Sodium 640 mg, Protein 33 g, Carbs 3 g, Fibre 1 g

Tandoori King Prawn Skewers

Prep Time: 9 minutes
Cooking Time: 6 minutes
Total Time: 15 minutes
Servings: 6
Difficulty: Not too tricky

INGREDIENTS

- 300 g king prawn
- 3 tbsp Greek yoghourt
- 2 tbsp tandoori masala spice blend powder
- 2 cloves garlic, crushed
- 1 lemon, ½ for the juice, ½ sliced into wedges for serving
- Spray oil

DIRECTIONS

1. Cut the skewer sticks down to size so that they can fit in the tray
2. In a bowl, mix the yoghurt, tandoori masala, garlic, and lemon juice.
3. Remove the excess water from the raw prawns with a paper towel.
4. Add the prawns to the bowl, and stir to coat.
5. Thread the prawns onto the kebab sticks. You can expect about 6 sticks of prawns.
6. Preheat the air fryer to a temperature of 200 °C/400 °F, add the prawns to the basket, and spray them with oil.
7. Cook the prawns in the air fryer for 8 minutes.

Nutrition Information

Calories 58, Fat 1 g, Saturates 1 g, Sugar 1 g, Sodium 291 mg, Protein 8 g, Carbs, 4 g, Fibre 1 g

Honey Glazed Salmon

Prep Time: 7 minutes
Cooking Time: 18 minutes
Total Time: 25 minutes
Servings: 4
Difficulty: Not too tricky

INGREDIENTS

- 0.75 salmon fillet
- Kosher salt, to taste
- Pepper, to taste
- ½ c honey-lime teriyaki sauce

DIRECTIONS

1. Remove the insert from the air fryer basket, and heat the air fryer to 200 °C/400 °F. Place a sheet of aluminium foil on top of the insert and place the salmon on top of that.
2. Season the salmon with ¼ tsp salt, then drizzle it with 2 tbsp of the teriyaki sauce.
3. Place the insert with the salmon on it in the air fryer basket and cook for approximately 15-18 minutes, basting the salmon every 5 minutes or so with the juices and sauce that have run down the sides of the fish. You want the fish to be opaque through and sticky on top.

Nutrition Information

Calories 270, Fat 7g, Saturates 2 g, Sodium 900 mg, Protein 36 g, Carbs 15 g, Fibre 1 g

Air Fryer Salmon Flatbreads

Prep Time: 9 minutes
Cooking Time: 6 minutes
Total Time: 15 minutes
Servings: 4
Difficulty: Not too tricky

INGREDIENTS

- 1 tbsp red wine vinegar
- 2 tbsp olive oil
- 1 tbsp capers, chopped
- 2 scallions, 1 finely chopped & 1 sliced thinly
- Kosher salt, to taste
- Pepper, to taste
- 1 pt grape tomatoes
- 0.5 kg skinless salmon fillet, cut into 3 cm pieces
- 1 tbsp flat leaf parsley, chopped
- 4 pieces naan bread
- 2 c baby arugula or kale
- Greek yoghourt, for serving

DIRECTIONS

1. In a small bowl, combine the red wine vinegar, 1 tbsp olive oil, capers, chopped scallion, and ¼ tsp pepper. Set aside.
2. Heat the air fryer to 200 °C/400 °F.
3. Toss the tomatoes and remaining tbsp oil with ¼ tsp salt and pepper each.
4. Season the salmon with ¼ tsp salt and pepper each.
5. Place the salmon fillet pieces in a single layer on the bottom of the air fryer basket. Add the tomatoes to the remaining space. Air fry until the salmon is opaque, approximately 6 minutes.
6. Transfer the tomatoes to a bowl with the vinegar-scallion mix and parsley.
7. Spread the yoghurt on the flatbreads, top them with salmon and arugula, then spoon the tomato mixture on top.

Nutrition Information

Calories 487, Fat 25 g, Saturates 9 g, Sodium 750 mg, Protein 41 g, Carbs 30 g, Fibre 10 g

Air Fryer Breaded Sea Scallops

Prep Time: 10 minutes
Cooking Time: 5 minutes
Total Time: 15 minutes
Servings: 4
Difficulty: Not too tricky

INGREDIENTS

- ½ c finely crushed buttery crackers
- ½ tsp garlic powder
- ½ tsp seafood seasoning
- 2 tbsp butter, melted
- 0.5 kg sea scallops, patted dry
- Cooking spray

DIRECTIONS

1. Preheat the air fryer to a temperature of 200 °C/400 °F.
2. Mix the cracker crumbs, garlic powder, and seafood seasoning in a small bowl. Place the butter in a separate shallow bowl.
3. Dip each scallop into the melted butter, followed by the bread coating.
4. Spray the air fryer basket with a layer of cooking spray, then arrange the scallops on the bottom of the basket so that they are spaced evenly from each other. You may need to cook them in separate batches.
5. Cook the scallops for 2 minutes, flip them over gently, then cook for another 2 minutes until they are opaque in colour.

Nutrition Information

Calories 282, Fat 18 g, Saturates 6 g, Sugar 1 g, Sodium 589 mg, Protein 17 g, Carbs 14 g

Air Fryer Crab Cakes

Prep Time: 15 minutes
Cooking Time: 10 minutes
Additional Time: 1 hour
Total Time: 1 hour 25 minutes
Servings: 4
Difficulty: Not too tricky

INGREDIENTS

- 1 large egg, beaten
- 2 tbsp mayonnaise
- 1 tsp Worcestershire sauce
- 1 tsp Dijon mustard
- 1 tsp seafood seasoning
- 1 tsp hot pepper sauce
- 2 tbsp green onion
- 0.5 kg crabmeat, drained and picked over
- 3 tbsp milk
- Salt, to taste
- Black pepper, to taste
- 11 saltine crackers, crushed
- 1 tsp baking powder
- 4 lemon wedges
- Cooking spray

DIRECTIONS

1. Combine the beaten eggs, mayonnaise, Worcestershire sauce, mustard, seafood seasoning, and hot sauce in a large bowl. Stir in the green onion and set aside.
2. Place the crab meat in a medium bowl and break it up with a fork. Add milk, salt, and pepper, then toss to coat. Add the saltine crumbs and baking powder, tossing to combine gently. Add the crab meat to the bowl with the egg mixture, careful not to break up the lumps of crab meat.
3. Form the crab meat into 8 patties by gently scooping with a 1/3 measuring cup. Place the patties on a plate and cover for 1 hour to 8 hours until the crab meat is firm.
4. Preheat the air fryer to a temperature of 200 °C/400 °F.
5. Spray the crab cakes with oil on both sides, then add them to the air fryer basket in a single layer. You may need to work in batches.
6. Cook the crab cakes in the air fryer for 5 minutes, flip them over gently, then cook for an additional 5 minutes.

Nutrition Information

Calories 242, Fat 9 g, Saturates 2 g,
Sugar 1 g, Sodium 937 mg, Protein 28 g,
Carbs 11 g, Fibre 1 g

Air Fryer Shrimp Scampi

Prep Time: 15 minutes
Cooking Time: 20 minutes
Total Time: 35 minutes
Servings: 4
Difficulty: Not too tricky

INGREDIENTS

- 340 g uncooked linguine
- ½ c dry white wine
- ¼ c unsalted butter
- 2 tbsp olive oil
- 1 tbsp + 1 tsp minced garlic
- 1 tsp crushed red pepper
- ½ tsp black pepper
- 1 ½ tsp kosher salt
- 0.5 kg large shrimp, peeled, deveined, tail-on
- 1 tsp grated lemon zest
- 2 tbsp lemon juice
- 1 tbsp minced fresh basil

DIRECTIONS

1. Cook pasta in a large boiling pot of generously salted water. Drain the pasta and transfer it into a bowl.
2. Place a cake pan in the air fryer basket, then preheat it to 200 °C/400 °F for 5 minutes.
3. Place the wine, butter, oil, garlic, and crushed red pepper in the pan. Cook the solution until the butter is melted and the wine is slightly reduced about 3-4 minutes.
4. Stir the black pepper and 1 tsp salt in a bowl, then add shrimp and toss to coat. Add the shrimp to the butter mixture in the pan, and toss it in the butter.
5. Cook the shrimp until fully cooked through, about 5 minutes.
6. Add the lemon zest, lemon juice, basil, and ½ tsp salt.
7. Add the shrimp to the pasta bowl and toss the shrimp scampi until it is evenly coated. Garnish with additional basil.

Nutrition Information

Calories 204, Fat 13 g, Saturates 6 g, Sugar 0 g, Sodium 976 mg, Protein 16 g, Carbs 3 g, Fibre 0 g

Air Fryer Tuna Steaks

Prep Time: 5 minutes
Cooking Time: 2 minutes
Total Time: 7 minutes
Servings: 2
Difficulty: Easy

INGREDIENTS

- 2 raw ahi tuna steaks
- 1 tbsp olive oil
- Salt, to taste
- pepper, to taste

Dipping Sauce:
- 2 green onions, thinly sliced
- 2 tbsp reduced-sodium soy sauce
- 1 tbsp lime juice
- 1 tbsp water
- ½ tsp minced garlic

DIRECTIONS

1. Preheat the air fryer to 185 °C/370 °F for 5 minutes.
2. Coat all sides of the tuna in olive oil, and season the tuna with salt and pepper.
3. Add the tuna steaks to the air fryer and cook for 2 minutes per side or until you have achieved your desired doneness.
4. Meanwhile, add the dipping sauce ingredients together in a small bowl for serving.

Nutrition Information

Calories 132, Fat 3 g, Saturates 0g, Sugar 3 g, Sodium 457 mg, Protein 21g, Carbs 5 g, Fibre 0 g

Air Fryer Haddock

Prep Time: 5 minutes
Cooking Time: 10 minutes
Total Time: 15 minutes
Servings: 3
Difficulty: Easy

INGREDIENTS

- 0.5 kg haddock fillets
- 1 egg
- ½ cup all-purpose flour
- 2 tsp paprika
- 1 c breadcrumbs
- ½ tsp garlic powder
- ½ tsp salt
- ¼ tsp pepper

DIRECTIONS

1. Place the breadcrumbs in one bowl, the eggs in another bowl, and the seasoning and flour in the final bowl.
2. Cut the haddock into serving-size pieces, and pat dry with a clean tea towel.
3. Dip each piece of fish into the flour-seasoning bowl, then shake off the excess. Dip the fish then into the egg, letting the excess egg drip off of the fish. Finally, dip the fish into the breadcrumbs, letting the excess shake off.
4. Preheat the air fryer to a temperature of 200 °C/400 °F.
5. Place the haddock in the air fryer basket, and spray it with cooking spray. Cook the fish for 10 minutes, flipping at the halfway point.

Nutrition Information

Calories 684, Fat 26 g, Saturates 8 g, Sugar 2 g, Sodium 1619 mg, Protein 36 g, Carbs 77 g, Fibre 8 g

Air Fryer Oysters

Prep Time: 10 minutes
Cooking Time: 8 minutes
Total Time: 18 minutes
Servings: 2
Difficulty: Not too tricky

INGREDIENTS

- 84 g jarred oysters
- ¼ c + ½ c flour
- ½ c cornmeal
- 1 egg
- ½ c milk
- 2 tsp salt
- ½ tsp paprika
- ¼ tsp cayenne
- ¼ tsp pepper
- ¼ tsp garlic powder
- Nonstick cooking spray

DIRECTIONS

1. Drain the jarred oysters and pat them dry.
2. Sprinkle the oysters with ¼ c flour, tossing to coat evenly. Shake off the excess flour.
3. Whisk together the egg and milk in one bowl. In a separate bowl, mix the cornmeal, remaining flour, and seasonings.
4. Dip each oyster into the egg mixture bowl, followed by the cornmeal-seasoning mixture bowl. Place the oysters on a baking sheet to rest while the air fryer is preheating.
5. Preheat the air fryer temperature to 200 °C/400 °F.
6. Spray the air fryer basket with a thin coat of cooking spray, then lay 4-6 oysters in the basket. Spray the oysters with cooking spray as well.
7. Ok, the oysters for 4 minutes, then flip them over. If you notice any chalky spots, add more cooking spray, then cook for an additional 4 minutes.

Nutrition Information

Calories 489, Fat 30 g, Saturates 6 g, Protein 55 g, Carbs 4 g, Fibre 0 g

Air Fryer Garlic Parmesan Shrimp

Prep Time: 5 minutes
Cooking Time: 10 minutes
Total Time: 15 minutes
Servings: 2
Difficulty: Not too tricky

INGREDIENTS

- 340 g frozen shrimp, thawed, deveined, and deshelled
- 1 tbsp olive oil
- 1 tbsp lemon juice
- ½ tsp salt
- ½ tsp black pepper
- ½ tsp garlic powder
- ½ tsp minced garlic
- ½ c shredded parmesan

DIRECTIONS

1. At the shrimp dry and place them in a medium bowl.
2. Add the olive oil, lemon juice, salt, pepper, garlic powder, minced garlic, and parmesan to the bowl, then mix well to coat the shrimp.
3. Add the shrimp to the air fryer basket in a single layer. You may have to cook the shrimp in batches. Cook for 10 minutes at 180 °C/360 °F, flipping the shrimp over at the halfway cooking time mark.

Nutrition Information

Calories 69, Fat 7 g, Saturates 1 g, Sugar 0 g, Sodium 555 mg, Protein 1 g, Carbs 2 g, Fibre 0 g

Air Fryer Crab Bites

Prep Time: 10 minutes
Cooking Time: 16 minutes
Total Time: 26 minutes
Servings: 6
Difficulty: Not too tricky

INGREDIENTS

- 0.5 kg imitation crab legs
- 3 tbsp melted butter
- Cajun seasoning
- Garlic butter dipping sauce, optional, for serving

DIRECTIONS

1. Cut the crab legs into 2 cm pieces.
2. In a medium-sized bowl, combine the crab, butter, and cajun seasoning. Mix to coat.
3. Add the crab to the air fryer in batches if necessary, as you want the crab to cook in a single layer. Set the air fryer temperature setting to 190 °C/380 °F, and cook the crab for 8 minutes. Shake the basket to mix everything well, then cook for an additional 8 minutes.

Nutrition Information

Calories 153, Fat 8 g, Saturates 5 g, Sugar 6 g, Sodium 1101 mg, Protein 6 g, Carbs 13 g,0 Fibre 1 g

Air Fryer Seafood Boil

Prep Time: 10 minutes
Cooking Time: 10 minutes
Total Time: 20 minutes
Servings: 1
Difficulty: Show off

INGREDIENTS

- 1 fresh corn cob, halved
- 0.25 kg shrimp
- 2 lobster tails, halved
- 2 tbsp butter
- Salt
- Black pepper
- Cajun seasoning

DIRECTIONS

1. Add the seafood boil components to the air fryer basket, including the butter and seasonings.
2. Set the temperature to 200 °C/400 °F and cook for 8-10 minutes, shaking frequently.

Nutrition Information

Calories 777, Fat 29 g, Saturates 15 g, Sugar 5 g, Sodium 1557 mg, Protein 103 g, Carbs 29 g, Fibre 3 g

Air Fryer Shrimp

Prep Time: 10 minutes
Cooking Time: 8 minutes
Total Time: 18 minutes
Servings: 4
Difficulty: Show off

INGREDIENTS

- 0.5 kg shrimp
- 1 garlic clove, minced
- 30 g unsalted butter, cut into cubes
- Salt, to taste
- Pepper, to taste
- Cooking oil spray
- Juice from ½ lemon

DIRECTIONS

1. Clean the shrimp, deveining and deshelling if desired. Transfer the shrimp into an oven-safe dish that will fit in your air fryer.
2. Season the shrimp with salt and pepper along with cooking oil. Stir to combine. Add cubed butter and place the shrimp in the air fryer basket inside the baking dish.
3. Cook the shrimp at 200 °C/400 °F for 8-10 minutes.
4. Add some lemon juice and chopped parsley to garnish, and enjoy.

Nutrition Information

Calories 169, Fat 8 g, Saturates 4 g, Sugar 1 g, Sodium 882 mg, Protein 23 g, Carbs 1 g, Fibre 1 g

White Fish with Garlic and Lemon Pepper

Prep Time: 5 minutes
Cooking Time: 12 minutes
Total Time: 17 minutes
Servings: 2
Difficulty: Not too tricky

INGREDIENTS

- 340 g tilapia fillets
- ½ tsp garlic powder
- ½ tsp lemon pepper seasoning
- ½ tsp onion powder
- Kosher salt
- Fresh cracked pepper
- Fresh chopped parsley

DIRECTIONS

1. Preheat the air fryer temperature setting to 180 °C/360 °F for 5 minutes.
2. Rinse and pat the fish fillets dry. Spray the fish with oil, then season them on both sides.
3. Lay a layer of parchment paper on the bottom of the air fryer. Spray the paper down with cooking spray to prevent sticking.
4. Lay the fish on the baking paper along with a few lemon wedges.
5. Air fry the fish for about 6-12 minutes or until the fish is flaky.
6. Sprinkle the fish with chopped parsley and serve with the toasted lemon wedges.

Nutrition Information

Calories 169, Fat 3 g, Saturates 1 g,
Sugar 1 g, Sodium 89 mg, Protein 34 g,
Carbs 1 g, Fibre 1 g

This page is for your notes

CHAPTER 3

FAMILY FAVOURITE RECIPES

Air Fryer Toad in a Hole

Prep Time: 5 minutes
Cooking Time: 25 minutes
Total Time: 30 minutes
Servings: 2
Difficulty: Show off

INGREDIENTS

- 4 pork sausages
- 1 tbsp vegetable oil
- 1 large egg
- 75 mL semi-skimmed milk
- 30 g plain flour, plus 2 tsp
- 25 g cornflour
- 100 g tenderstem broccoli
- 100 g green beans, trimmed
- 100 g frozen peas
- 200 mL beef or chicken stock
- 10 g butter

DIRECTIONS

1. Preheat the air fryer temperature to 200 °C/400 °F.
2. Add a paper liner to the inner edge of the air fryer basket and drizzle a layer of oil.
3. Add the sausages to the air fryer and cook for 5-7 minutes or until they are just beginning to show some colour.
4. While the sausages are cooking, make a batter consisting of egg, milk, flour, and cornflour. Mix the batter until it is completely smooth. Add a dash of salt and pepper, then let the batter rest.
5. Remove the air fryer basket from the air fryer, turn over the sausages, and quickly pour the batter over them. Return the basket back into the air fryer and cook for 15 minutes. When it is done, the batter will be dark golden brown and crispy in texture. Don't check on the contents of the air fryer before this, as the batter could sink. If the batter is not dark golden brown, only cook for an additional 2-3 minutes or so.
6. While the toad-in-the-hole is cooking, make the gravy. Add the stock into a small saucepan, and whisk the flour in evenly. Bring the gravy to a low simmer on medium heat, then add the butter and season it with black pepper. Cook the gravy for 4-6 minutes, until thickened. You can then reduce the temperature to the lowest setting in order to keep it warm until it's time to drown your plate in gravy.
7. You can then add your broccoli, green beans, and peas to a bowl and steam them in the microwave for 2 -3 minutes until the vegetables are completely cooked through.
8. When it is time to assemble your plate, use a spatula to gently lift the toad in a hole from the air fryer and cut it into portions; add a generous serving of the vegetables and gravy, and you are all set.

Nutrition Information

Calories 604, Fat37g, Saturates 12 g,
Sugar 6 g, Sodium 2.3 g, Protein 26.1 g,
Carbs 39.6 g, Fibre 4.7 g

Air Fryer Shepherd's Pie

Prep Time: 20 minutes
Cooking Time: 20 minutes
Total Time: 40 minutes
Servings: 4
Difficulty: Show off

INGREDIENTS

Mashed Potato Topping
- 2 cups prepared instant mashed potatoes
- ½ cup milk
- 3 tbsp butter, melted
- ½ cup cheddar cheese, shredded, optional

Filling
- 1 medium onion, chopped
- 2 cloves garlic, minced
- 0.5 kg ground beef or lamb
- 1 cup frozen vegetables
- 1 packet brown gravy mix (3 tbsp)
- 2 tsp Worcestershire sauce
- ½ tsp dried thyme leaves

DIRECTIONS

1. Combine the beef/lamb, onion and garlic in a large skillet. Cook over medium-high heat until all of the meat is completely browned and no pink remains.
2. Add the frozen vegetables, gravy mix packet, Worcestershire sauce, thyme leaves, and 1 cup of water to the skillet. Bring the filling mixture to a boil and simmer for 7-9 minutes on medium-high heat.
3. Preheat the air fryer temperature to 190 °C/380 °F.
4. Place the beef mixture in the bottom of an air fryer/heat-safe pan.
5. In a separate bowl, prepare the mashed potato topping. Mix together the mashed potatoes, milk, melted butter, and cheddar cheese (optional). Stir the potato topping until well incorporated.
6. Spread the potato mixture on top of the beef filling in the air fryer-safe pan. Place the pan in the air fryer for 10-15 minutes, until the whole shepherd's pie is heated through and the top is golden-coloured.

Nutrition Information

Calories 601, Fat 37 g, Saturates 17 g, Sugar 3 g, Sodium 305 mg, Protein 29 g, Carbs 40 g, Fibre 4 g

Air Fryer Crumpets

Prep Time: 0 minutes
Cooking Time: 3 minutes
Total Time: 3 minutes
Servings: 2
Difficulty: Easy

INGREDIENTS

- 4 frozen crumpets
- 2 tsp butter
- 2 tsp jam (optional)
- 2 tsp soft cheese (optional)
- 2 tsp chicken liver pate (optional)

DIRECTIONS

1. Place up to 4 crumpets in the air fryer basket, ensuring that none are touching or crowding each other. Set the air fryer to 180 °C/360 °F, then cook for 2 minutes.
2. After the 2-minute timer goes up, add a spread of butter to each of the crumpets, and push the air fryer basket back into the air fryer for 1 more minute of cooking.
3. Serve as the butter drips down the delicious crumpet holes.

Nutrition Information

Calories 346, Fat 8 g, Saturates 4 g, Sugar 4 g, Sodium 586 mg, Protein 10 g, Carbs 58 g, Fibre 3 g

Air Fryer Bubble and Squeak

Prep Time: 5 minutes
Cooking Time: 12 minutes
Total Time: 17 minutes
Servings: 2
Difficulty: Not too tricky

INGREDIENTS

- 500 g mashed potatoes
- 200 g cooked cabbage
- 100 g meat, optional
- 30 g grated cheddar cheese
- 2 tsp thyme
- Salt, to taste
- Pepper, to taste

DIRECTIONS

1. Place all ingredients into a mixing bowl. Mix the ingredients well and form them into a ball.
2. Load the ball into your air fryer with a cake or baking pan that will fit inside the basket or tray. Air fry the pan for 8 minutes on heat 180 °C/360 °F, followed by an additional 4 minutes at a heat of 200 °C/400 °F.
3. When your timer goes off, you are ready to dig in. Simple as that.

Nutrition Information

Calories 1067, Fat 10 g, Saturates 5 g, Sugar 12 g, Sodium 423 mg, Protein 40 g, Carbs 209 g, Fibre 19 g

Air Fryer Cheese Flan

Prep Time: 10 minutes
Cooking Time: 17 minutes
Total Time: 27 minutes
Servings: 8
Difficulty: Not too tricky

INGREDIENTS

- Pie crust
- ½ small onion, diced
- 4 large eggs
- 120 mL semi-skimmed milk
- 180 g grated cheese
- 2 tsp parsley
- Salt, to taste
- Pepper, to taste

DIRECTIONS

1. Add your shortcrust pastry or pie crust to the tart tin.
2. Poke holes in the bottom of the pastry with a fork to let it breathe while baking.
3. Add the sliced onion to the bottom of the flan.
4. Mix your eggs, milk, and seasoning in a separate bowl and beat until mixed thoroughly. Add the cheese to the mix, too.
5. Pour the cheese-egg mixture over the sliced onion in the tart tin.
6. Place the cheese flan into the air fryer, and set the temperature to 160 °C/320 °F. Cook the cheese flan for 17 minutes or until a toothpick comes out clean.

Nutrition Information

Calories 136, Fat 9 g, Saturates 4 g, Sugar 1 g, Sodium 432 mg, Protein 10 g, Carbs 4 g, Fibre 0 g

Air Fryer Frittata

Prep Time: 10 minutes
Cooking Time: 39 minutes
Total Time: 49 minutes
Servings: 8
Difficulty: Not too tricky

INGREDIENTS

- Large eggs
- 240 mL mascarpone
- 200 g grated reduced-fat cheddar cheese
- 6 reduced fat sausages, cut into quarters
- 1 large sweet potato
- 1 medium zucchini
- 1 tbsp extra virgin olive oil
- 2 spring onions, sliced
- 1 tsp parsley
- Salt, to taste
- Pepper, to taste
- Sliced cherry tomatoes, optional

DIRECTIONS

1. Prep the vegetables: peel and dice your sweet potato into cubes. Slice the zucchini into medium slices, then into quarters. Add the extra virgin olive oil, salt, pepper, and parsley to the bowl, and mix the vegetables and seasonings together with your hands.
2. Load the sweet potatoes and zucchini into the air fryer basket, set at 180 °C/360 °F, and air fry them together for 5 minutes.
3. Shake the air fryer basket and add the sausages on top of the vegetables. Cook them for an additional 12 minutes.
4. Load the sweet potatoes, zucchini, and sausages into the silicone dishes in addition to spring onions.
5. In a medium bowl, crack the eggs and beat the eggs with a fork. Add the cream, salt, pepper, and parsley to the eggs.
6. Add the grated cheese to the silicone mould, then pour the egg mixture on top. Decorate the top with cherry tomatoes (optional), and place the mould back into the air fryer at the same temperature for 17 minutes. Check on the frittata when your timer goes off, then set the air fryer to 170 °C/340 °F and cook for an additional 5 minutes. Once the frittata is cool enough to remove from the mould, you can pop it out and enjoy.

Nutrition Information

Calories 414, Fat 30 g, Saturates 13 g, Sugar 3 g, Sodium 902 mg, Protein 24 g, Carbs 11 g, Fibre 1 g

Air Fryer Breakfast Potatoes

Prep Time: 5 minutes
Cooking Time: 12 minutes
Total Time: 17 minutes
Servings: 2
Difficulty: Not too tricky

INGREDIENTS

- 1 potato, diced
- 1 red bell pepper, diced
- 1 red onion, diced
- 1 tbsp olive oil
- 1 tsp garlic powder
- ¼ tsp salt
- ½ tsp smoked paprika

DIRECTIONS

1. Brush the air fryer rack with oil, and preheat to 190 °C/375 °F.
2. Dice the potatoes, then transfer them to a bowl. Top with olive oil, garlic powder, paprika, salt, pepper, and any other seasonings of your liking (parsley, onion powder, etc).
3. Place the diced potatoes in the air fryer and spread the potatoes evenly in a single layer. Cook for 8 minutes, flipping them over halfway through the cooking time.
4. Add the diced red bell pepper and onion, then cook for 4-5 more minutes.

Nutrition Information

Calories 188, Fat 7 g, Saturates 1 g, Sugar 6 g, Sodium 303 mg, Protein 4 g, Carbs 29 g, Fibre 5 g

Air Fryer Roast Dinner

Prep Time: 15 minutes
Cooking Time: 45 minutes
Additional Time: 30 minutes
Total Time: 1 hour 30 minutes
Servings: 2
Difficulty: Show off

INGREDIENTS

- 2-3 medium potatoes, peeled and quartered
- 3 tsp vegetable oil or other alternatives
- 1 large or 2 small chicken breasts, skin on
- 3 medium carrots, peeled and thickly sliced
- 100 g frozen peas
- Gravy, to serve

DIRECTIONS

1. Soak the quartered potatoes in water for 30 minutes, then drain and rinse them off. Dry off the potatoes thoroughly, dump them in a bowl, and drizzle 1 tsp oil over them with salt and pepper seasoning. Coat the potatoes in oil and seasoning, and add them to the air fryer basket.
2. Heat the air fryer up to 190 °C/380 °F and cook the potatoes for 10 minutes.
3. While the potatoes are cooking, coat the chicken with 1 tsp of oil and some salt and pepper for taste. Once the 10-minute potato timer has gone up, move the potatoes to the perimeter of the air fryer basket and lay the chicken breasts in the middle. Cook the chicken for 10 minutes.
4. While the chicken and potatoes are cooking together, coat the carrots in the final tsp of oil. When the timer has sounded off, remove the chicken from the air fryer basket and add the carrots into the mix. Mix the potatoes and carrots together, then press them up against the sides of the basket again. Replace the chicken in the centre of the basket. Cook the potatoes, carrots, and chicken for an additional 10-15 minutes.
5. The chicken should be thoroughly cooked, but you can double-check with a meat thermometer (it should read 70 °C). If it isn't done, cook a bit longer in 5-minute spurts.
6. Put peas in a small, ovenproof dish with 2 tbsp water and cover it with foil in order to prevent moisture from evaporating in the air fryer. Place the dish in the centre of the air fryer basket, and cook for a final 10 minutes.
7. The potatoes should be golden and crisp, and the carrots should be soft.
8. Enjoy this roast with the vegetables and gravy.

Nutrition Information

Calories 444, Fat 13 g, Saturates 2 g,
Sugar 12 g, Sodium 0 g, Protein 36 g,
Carbs 41 g, Fibre 10 g

Yorkshire Parkin

Prep Time: 10 minutes
Cooking Time: 25 minutes
Total Time: 35 minutes
Servings: 12
Difficulty: Not too tricky

INGREDIENTS

- 250 g plain flour
- 200 g oats
- 2 tsp baking powder
- 3 tsp ground ginger
- 1 tsp cinnamon
- 1 tsp mixed spice
- 1 pinch salt
- 150 mL milk
- 150 g butter
- 150 g brown sugar
- 100 g treacle or molasses
- 200 g golden syrup

DIRECTIONS

1. Grease and line a casserole dish or cake tin that will fit in the basket of your air fryer.
2. Preheat your air fryer to 170 °C/350 °F.
3. Throw your oats in a food processor or blender until they are a finer texture. Mix the oats, flour, baking powder, spices, and salt in a bowl.
4. Heat and melt the brown sugar, golden syrup, treacle, milk, and butter in a bowl, then give a good mix.
5. Pour the wet ingredients into the bowl with the dry ingredients.
6. Pour the batter into the dish you prepared and pop it in the air fryer for approximately 25 minutes or until a toothpick comes out clean. If you think the cake is too brown, you can cover it with foil at some point during the baking.

Nutrition Information

Calories 363, Fat 12 g, Saturates 7 g, Sugar 33 g, Sodium 169 mg, Protein 5 g, Carbs 61 g, Fibre 3 g

English Pancakes

Prep Time: 5 minutes
Cooking Time: 10 minutes
Total Time: 15 minutes
Servings: 6
Difficulty: Easy

INGREDIENTS

- 30 g sugar
- 360 mL milk
- 2 medium eggs
- ½ tbsp vegetable oil
- ½ tsp vanilla extract
- 160 g plain flour
- Spray oil

DIRECTIONS

1. Blend the sugar, milk, eggs, vegetable oil, and vanilla extract in a bowl. Add the flour 1 spoonful at a time, mixing between each spoonful. Blend until no lumps remain.
2. Line the bottom basket of the air fryer with baking paper.
3. Place 1 tbsp of the mixture in each corner of the air fryer basket on top of the paper. You want the batter to be thin and runny in order to achieve the classic English pancake consistency.
4. Set the air fryer temperature to 200 °C/400 °F and cook for 5 minutes, flipping halfway through. Repeat until all of the batter has been used.
5. Top your pancakes with your favourite garnishes or toppings.

Nutrition Information

Calories 185, Fat 5 g, Saturates 3 g, Sugar 8 g, Sodium 47 mg, Protein 6 g, Carbs 28 g, Fibre 1 g

Air Fryer Black Pudding

Prep Time: 0 minutes
Cooking Time: 9 minutes
Total Time: 9 minutes
Servings: 2
Difficulty: Easy

INGREDIENTS

- Black Pudding Slices

DIRECTIONS

1. If your black pudding is being cooked from frozen, place the roll in the air fryer for 6 minutes at 80 °C/160 °F to make the black pudding roll soft enough to slice.
2. Remove the roll from the air fryer and slice off the black pudding slices that you want to eat.
3. Place the slices in the air fryer at 180 °C/360 °F, or 9 minutes, ensuring that they do not overlap.

Nutrition Information

Calories 297, Fat 22 g, Saturates 9 g, Sugar 0 g, Sodium 2 g, Protein 5 g, Carbs 9 g, Fibre 0 g

Air Fryer English Breakfast

Prep Time: 3 minutes
Cooking Time: 15 minutes
Total Time: 18 minutes
Servings: 2
Difficulty: Show off

INGREDIENTS

- 6 English sausages
- 6 bacon rashers
- 2 large tomatoes
- 4 black pudding
- 1/2can baked beans
- 2 large eggs
- 1 tbsp whole milk
- 1 tsp butter
- Salt, to taste
- Pepper, to taste

DIRECTIONS

1. Crack your eggs into a ramekin and add the butter, milk, salt, and pepper. Place this in the air fryer. Add to the air fryer basket the bacon rashers, sausages, and black pudding. Slice the tomatoes in half, and season the tops with a light dash of salt and pepper.
2. Close the air fryer basket, making sure that there is enough room for each of the items to cook. Set the temperature setting of the air fryer to 180 °C/360 °F, and cook the breakfast set for 10 minutes. At the 5-minute mark, however, stir the eggs with a fork.
3. When your 10-minute timer has gone off, check to make sure that the eggs are scrambled to your liking, and remove them from the air fryer. This will be hot, so wear a kitchen mitt. Replace the ramekin space with one of the cold-baked beans. Cook the entire air fryer basket for an additional 5 minutes.

Nutrition Information

Calories 1496, Fat 124 g, Saturates 42 g, Sugar 4 g, Sodium 3005 mg, Protein 70 g, Carbs 22 g, Fibre 6 g

Air Fryer Egg and Bacon Pie

Prep Time: 10 minutes
Cooking Time: 20 minutes
Total Time: 30 minutes
Servings: 8
Difficulty: Not too tricky

INGREDIENTS

- Pie Crust
- Bacon, cooked
- 9 large eggs
- 4 tbsp skim milk
- 2 tsp parsley
- Salt, to taste
- Pepper, to taste
- Flour for dusting
- 1 small egg, beaten

DIRECTIONS

1. Slice the bacon into chunks.
2. Line a quiche dish with your pie crust or shortcrust pastry. Add your bacon bits to the bottom of the pie crust. Spread the bacon evenly for an even distribution of bacon in the pie.
3. In a bowl, add the eggs and seasoning. Beat them together until well-mixed, then add the milk.
4. Pour the egg and milk mixture over the slices of bacon until the quiche dish is almost full.
5. Add the top layer of your shortcrust pastry over the egg and bacon pie.
6. Brush the pastry with egg wash, and poke a few holes in the centre of the pastry. This will allow the pastry to breathe while it cooks.
7. Load the pie into the air fryer. Set the temperature to 170 °C/340 °F, and cook for 20 minutes. Leave the pie in the air fryer to set for an additional 20 minutes.

Nutrition Information

Calories 484, Fat 30 g, Saturates 10g, Sugar 1 g, Sodium 757 mg, Protein 20g, Carbs 2 g, Fibre 2 g

Lancashire Hot Pot

Prep Time: 20 minutes
Cooking Time: 1 hour 12 minutes
Total Time: 1 hour 32 minutes
Servings: 4
Difficulty: Show off

INGREDIENTS

- 100 g butter
- 900 g stewing lamb, cut into large chunks
- 3 lamb kidneys, sliced, fat removed
- 2 medium onions, chopped
- 4 carrots, peeled and sliced
- 25 g plain flour
- 2 tsp Worcestershire sauce
- 500 mL lamb or chicken stock
- 2 bay leaves
- 900 g potatoes, peeled and sliced

DIRECTIONS

1. Heat the air fryer to 140 °C/280 °F.
2. On the stovetop, heat the butter in a large ovenproof pot or Dutch oven and brown the stewing lamb in batches, followed by the kidneys. Set the meat aside.
3. Fry the onions and carrots in the pan with a little more butter until they are golden in colour.
4. Sprinkle the flour over the vegetables, allowing them to cook for a couple of minutes, then shake the Worcestershire sauce and stock over the mixture. Bring it to a boil.
5. Stir in the stewing lamb, kidneys, and bay leaves, then turn off the heat.
6. Arrange the potatoes on top of the lamb and drizzle more butter on top.
7. Cover the pot, then place it in the air fryer for 1 hour 12 minutes, or until the potatoes are cooked.
8. Remove the lid, brush the potatoes with more butter, then brown the potatoes in the air fryer for 5 or so minutes without the lid on the pot.

Nutrition Information

Calories 993, Fat 56 g, Saturates 26 g, Sugar 12 g, Sodium 1430 mg, Protein 70 g, Carbs 56 g, Fibre 7 g

Air Fryer Scotch Eggs

Prep Time: 15 minutes
Cooking Time: 15 minutes
Total Time: 30 minutes
Servings: 6
Difficulty: Show off

INGREDIENTS

Dipping Sauce:
- 3 tbsp Greek yoghourt
- 2 tbsp mango chutney
- 1 tbsp mayonnaise
- ⅛ tsp salt
- ⅛ tsp pepper
- ⅛ tsp curry powder
- ⅛ tsp cayenne (optional)

Scotch Eggs:
- 0.5 kg pork sausage
- 6 eggs, hard-boiled and shelled
- 1/3 cup flour
- 2 eggs, lightly beaten
- 1 cup breadcrumbs

DIRECTIONS

1. Prepare the dipping sauce by combining the yoghurt, mango chutney, mayonnaise, salt, pepper, curry powder, and cayenne in a small bowl. Refrigerate the dipping sauce until you are ready to use it.
2. Divide the pork sausage into 6 even portions, then flatten them into a thin patty. Place one hard-boiled egg in the middle of each patty, and wrap the pork patty around the egg, enclosing it completely.
3. Preheat the air fryer temperature to 200 °C/400 °F.
4. Add flour to a small bowl, the two beaten eggs to a different bowl, and breadcrumbs to a plate. This is your breading station. Dip each sausage-wrapped egg into the flour, covering it on all sides, followed by the beaten egg. Let the excess egg run off, then roll each ball into the plate of panko breadcrumbs.
5. Spray the air fryer basket with a thin layer of oil. Arrange the eggs in the fryer basket such that they are not overcrowded and are laying in a single layer. You may need to cook your eggs in batches.
6. Cook the eggs for 12 minutes, turning the eggs over halfway through the cooking time.
7. Serve the scotch eggs with dipping sauce.

Nutrition Information

Calories 407, Fat 28 g, Saturates 9 g, Sugar 3 g, Sodium 945 mg, Protein, 21 g, Carbs 22 g, Fibre 0 g

Air Fryer Gammon Steak (Ham Steak)

Prep Time: 5 minutes
Cooking Time: 8 minutes
Total Time: 13 minutes
Servings: 2
Difficulty: Easy

INGREDIENTS

- 1 tbsp honey
- 2 tsp mustard
- 2 tsp olive oil
- 2 gammon steaks or ham steaks
- Cooking spray
- 2 eggs, optional
- 4 pineapple rings, optional

DIRECTIONS

1. Prepare the glaze by mixing the olive oil, honey, and mustard.
2. Pat the gammon steaks dry with paper towels and brush them with the glaze on both sides. If you are cooking pineapple rings, brush them with the glaze as well.
3. Preheat the air fryer to 180 °C/350 °F. Place the steaks and pineapple rings in the air fryer and cook for 4-5 minutes.
4. Flip the steaks and pineapples over and brush them with glaze once more. Cook for a further 4-5 minutes.
5. If you are also making eggs, you can place them in silicone moulds with cooking spray and set them on top of the steaks. When cooking, make sure that the egg white is set before removing them from the air fryer.

Nutrition Information

Calories 433, Fat 16 g, Saturates 3 g, Sugar 21 g, Sodium 2247 mg, Protein 50 g, Carbs 22 g, Fibre 0 g

Air Fryer Soft Boiled Eggs

Prep Time: 0 minutes
Cooking Time: 10 minutes
Total Time: 10 minutes
Servings: 3
Difficulty: Easy

INGREDIENTS

- 6 large eggs
- Sea salt

DIRECTIONS

1. The air fryer basket after ensuring that none are cracked.
2. Set the air fryer temperature to 120 °C/250 °F. Cook the eggs for 10 minutes.
3. Quickly load the eggs into egg cups immediately after the timer goes off and slice off the tops of the eggs.

Nutrition Information

Calories 126, Fat 8 g, Saturates 3 g,
Sugar 1 g, Sodium 125 mg, Protein 11 g,
Carbs 1 g, Fibre 0 g

Welsh Rarebit

Prep Time: 2 minutes
Cooking Time: 5 minutes
Total Time: 7 minutes
Servings: 4
Difficulty: Easy

INGREDIENTS

- 8 slices bread
- 1 egg
- 200 g cheddar cheese, grated
- 2 tbsp Worcestershire sauce
- 1 tsp Dijon mustard
- 2 tbsp whole milk

DIRECTIONS

1. In a bowl, combine the egg, cheese, Worcestershire sauce, dijon mustard, and whole milk.
2. Toast the sliced bread in the air fryer at 180 °C/360 °F for 2-3 minutes.
3. Divide the cheese mixture among the slices and spread it evenly over the bread.
4. Add the bread back to the air fryer for 6-8 minutes, until the cheese has melted and browned.

Nutrition Information

Calories 343, Fat 18 g, Saturates 11 g,
Sugar 5 g, Sodium 719 mg, Protein 20 g,
Carbs 28 g, Fibre 2 g

Mince Pies

Prep Time: 15 minutes
Cooking Time: 15 minutes
Total Time: 30 minutes
Servings: 12
Difficulty: Not too tricky

INGREDIENTS

- 1 sheet shortcrust pastry
- Flour
- 300 g mincemeat
- 1 egg

DIRECTIONS

1. Unroll the shortcrust pastry and lightly dust a 6-hole muffin tray. Use a pastry cutter to cut a circle shape that is slightly bigger than the muffin hole. The idea is that you will push the pastry in, and it will fill up the hope to the brim.
2. Add the mincemeat to the pastry, ¾ full.
3. Use the leftover shortcrust pastry to make a lid. If you are going for a closed pie, be sure to poke holes in it to let it breathe while cooking.
4. Whisk an egg, then use a brush to apply an egg glaze over the pies.
5. Place the baking tin in the air fryer and cook at 180 °C/350 °F for 10 minutes; check on the pies, then cook for an additional 5 minutes.

Nutrition Information

Calories 168, Fat 2 g, Saturates 1 g,
Sugar 17 g, Sodium 286 mg, Protein 3 g,
Carbs 34 g, Fibre 1 g

Chicken Pot Pie

Prep Time: 5 minutes
Cooking Time: 17 minutes
Total Time: 22 minutes
Servings: 4
Difficulty: Show off

INGREDIENTS

- 1 sheet puff pastry
- 3 chicken thighs
- Leftover veggies
- 3 tbsp frozen peas
- 2 tbsp semi-skimmed milk
- 2 tbsp cream cheese
- 1 tsp white wine
- Egg wash
- Cooking spray

DIRECTIONS

1. Roll the pie crust or puff pastry out and cut out the same size as your ramekins. Spray the ramekins with olive oil spray to prevent sticking.
2. Place the raw chicken thighs in the air fryer and season with salt, pepper, and parsley. Air fry for 10 minutes at a temperature of 180 °C/360 °F.
3. When the air fryer has finished cooking the chicken, dice it up and mix it with the leftover veggies, cream cheese, white wine, and milk. Add the frozen peas and mix again.
4. Load the chicken pot pie filling into the ramekins, then cover them with the puff pastry. Poke a hole or snip a gash in the top of the pies to let them breathe during cooking. Brush the tops with an egg wash.
5. Bake the ramekins in the air fryer for 17 minutes until the pies are golden brown on top and piping hot inside.

Nutrition Information

Calories 562, Fat 40 g, Saturates 11 g,
Sugar 2 g, Sodium 245 mg, Protein 20 g,
Carbs 30 g, Fibre 1 g

This page is for your notes

CHAPTER 4

POULTRY RECIPES

Air Fryer Chicken Wings

Prep Time: 5 minutes
Cooking Time: 25 minutes
Total Time: 30 minutes
Servings: 3
Difficulty: Not too tricky

INGREDIENTS

- 1 kg chicken wings
- 1 tbsp olive oil
- ½ tsp garlic powder
- ½ tsp onion powder
- ½ tsp paprika
- ½ tsp salt
- ½ tsp black pepper

DIRECTIONS

1. Preheat the air fryer to a temperature of 180 °C/360 °F.
2. Prepare the chicken wings by patting them dry with a kitchen roll or tea towel. The drier the chicken wings are, the crispier they will come out.
3. Add all of the seasonings, and be sure that all of the wings are coated evenly.
4. Add the seasoned chicken wings to the air fryer. Depending on the size and how many wings you are cooking, you may need to cook them in evenly-sized batches. The key is to make sure that the wings are not touching each other in the air fryer basket. This will make your wings nice and crispy.
5. Cook the chicken wings for 20 minutes, turning or shaking them in the basket 2-3 times during the cooking time.
6. Increase the temperature to 200 °C/400 °F and cook the wings for an additional 5 minutes until the skin meets its peak crispiness.
7. These chicken wings are best paid with BBQ sauce, Hot Pepper Sauce, or Buffalo Sauce.

Nutrition Information

Calories 853, Fat 64 g, Saturates 22 g,
Sugar 1 g, Sodium 1274 mg, Protein 42 g,
Carbs 25 g, Fibre 1 g

Whole Chicken Air Fryer

Prep Time: 5 minutes
Cooking Time: 1 hour
Total Time: 1 hour 5 minutes
Servings: 4-6
Difficulty: Easy

INGREDIENTS

- 1 whole chicken, up to 2kg, depending on your air fryer size
- 1 tbsp olive oil
- 1 tsp smoked paprika
- 1 tsp dried mixed herbs
- 1 tsp garlic powder

DIRECTIONS

1. With a brush, coat the entire chicken in olive oil.
2. Mix the seasoning together and spread it on the chicken in an even layer. If there isn't enough spice mix because you have a bigger chicken, make up some more using the same ratios.
3. Place the whole chicken in the air fryer basket, breast-side down. Cook at 180 °C/360 °F for 45 minutes. During the cooking time, check on it once or twice to make sure that it is not drying out or burning.
4. At the 45-minute mark, flip the chicken over so that it is breast-side up and set an additional 15-minute timer.
5. After the full hour of cooking, check that the chicken has cooked through with a meat thermometer. If the chicken is not cooked through, replace it in the air fryer and check on it in 5-minute increments until the juice runs clear and the meat temperature is adequate.

Nutrition Information

Calories 390, Fat 24 g, Saturates 6 g, Sugar 0 g, Sodium 23 mg, Protein 41 g, Carbs 1 g, Fibre 0 g

Air Fryer Chicken Breasts

Prep Time: 10 minutes
Cooking Time: 20 minutes
Additional Time: 5 minutes
Total Time: 35 minutes
Servings: 4
Difficulty: Easy

INGREDIENTS

- 1 chicken breast
- ½ tbsp olive oil
- ½ tsp salt
- ½ tsp black pepper
- ½ tsp garlic powder
  (or alternative seasoning of your choice)

DIRECTIONS

1. Preheat the air fryer to 180 °C/360 °F.
2. Brush or spray each chicken breast with oil.
3. Season one side of each breast.
4. Place each chicken breast, smooth side down, into the air fryer basket. Season the other side as well.
5. Set the timer for 10 minutes.
6. After the 10-minute marker, flip over the chicken breasts in order for them to cook evenly on both sides.
7. After the full 20-minute cook time, check that the chicken is cooked completely using a meat thermometer.
8. Leave the chicken to rest for 5 minutes before slicing and serving.

Nutrition Information

Calories 266, Fat 11 g, Saturates 2 g, Sugar 0 g, Sodium 1253 g, Protein 38 g, Carbs 2 g, Fibre 0 g

Air Fryer Chicken Drumsticks

Prep Time: 5 minutes
Cooking Time: 25 minutes
Total Time: 30 minutes
Servings: 8
Difficulty: Easy

INGREDIENTS

- 8-12 chicken drumsticks
- Seasonings
- Oil (optional)

DIRECTIONS

1. Preheat the air fryer to a 200 °C/400 °F temperature.
2. Optionally, brush the drumsticks with oil.
3. Season your drumsticks with your favourite seasoning or spices. Salt is also okay if you prefer.
4. Place the drumsticks in the air fryer basket. You may need to cook them in batches to make sure that the drumsticks are not touching the basket and are able to cook evenly.
5. Cook for 22-25 minutes, flipping the drumsticks over halfway through the cooking time.
6. After your timer, make sure that the chicken drumsticks are cooked all the way through (75 °C with a meat thermometer).

Nutrition Information

Calories 533, Fat26 g, Saturates7 g, Sugar 0 g, Sodium363 mg, Protein 66 g, Carbs 0 g, Fibre 0 g

Air Fryer Chicken Thighs

Prep Time: 5 minutes
Cooking Time: 25 minutes
Total Time: 30 minutes
Servings: 4
Difficulty: Easy / Not too tricky / Show off

INGREDIENTS

- 1 kg chicken thighs
- 2 tsp seasoning

DIRECTIONS

1. Preheat the air fryer to 200 °C/400 °F.
2. Pat the chicken thighs dry with some kitchen roll, then season.
3. Put the seasoned chicken thighs into the air fryer. Depending on the size of the air fryer basket that you have, you may need to cook them in batches.
4. Cook the drumsticks in the air fryer for 10 minutes. After your 10-minute timer goes up, turn the chicken thighs over and cook for an additional 10 minutes. The thighs should be cooked through and crispy. If this isn't the case, cook the thighs in 5-minute increments until they are cooked through.

Nutrition Information

Calories 213, Fat 16 g, Saturates 4 g, Sodium 263 mg, Protein 16 g, Carbs 2 g

Air Fryer Hunters Chicken

Prep Time: 5 minutes
Cooking Time: 25 minutes
Total Time: 30 minutes
Servings: 2
Difficulty: Not too tricky

INGREDIENTS

- 2 chicken breasts
- 4 rashers of bacon
- 6 tbsp BBQ sauce
- 50 g grated cheese (mozzarella, gouda, or parmesan suggested)

DIRECTIONS

1. Preheat the air fryer to 190° C/380 °F.
2. Place the chicken breasts in the bottom of the air fryer basket and set a timer for 10 minutes. Turn the chicken breasts over halfway through, at 5 minutes. If you have a small air fryer, you may need to cook your chicken in batches.
3. After 10 minutes in the fryer, remove the chicken breasts with tongs or a fork. Wrap each breast with two rashers of bacon. You can use cocktail sticks to help hold the bacon in place.
4. Return the bacon-wrapped chicken breasts to the air fryer basket for an additional 10 minutes, turning again at the halfway mark.
5. At the end of the cooking time, open the air fryer basket and brush BBQ sauce evenly across both chicken breasts and sprinkle grated cheese on top.
6. Replace the basket into the air fryer for 2-3 more minutes to melt the cheese and heat up the BBQ sauce on top of the chicken breasts.
7. After the last stage of cooking, remove the chicken breasts from the air fryer. Check that the chicken is cooked all the way through with a meat thermometer.

Nutrition Information

Calories 575, Fat27 g, Saturates 11 g, Sugar17 g, Sodium1454 mg, Protein57 g, Carbs22 g, Fibre 0 g

Air Fryer Chicken Fajitas

Prep Time: 5 minutes
Cooking Time: 15 minutes
Total Time: 20 minutes
Servings: 4
Difficulty: Not too tricky

INGREDIENTS

- 6 chicken thighs or 4 chicken breasts
- 1 onion, chopped
- 3 sweet peppers, deseeded and sliced
- 2 tbsp fajita spice mix*
- 1 tbsp olive oil
- 1 tbsp chipotle paste (optional)
- Juice from ½ a lime

DIRECTIONS

1. Slice the chicken into strips.
2. Mix the oil, fajita spice, chipotle paste, and lime juice into a bowl.
3. Add the chicken strips into the bowl and turn to coat. Leave the chicken in the bowl for at least 10 minutes to marinate.
4. While the chicken is marinating, you can prepare the onions and peppers.
5. Preheat the air fryer to a temperature of 200 °C/400 °F.
6. Transfer the chicken to the air fryer basket and cook for 10 minutes, shaking the basket at the halfway mark.
7. Add the vegetables to the chicken in the air fryer basket and stir thoroughly. Replace the basket back into the air fryer and cook for an additional 5 minutes.

*If you don't have access to the fajita spice mix, you can make your own:

- 2 tsp ground cumin
- 2 tsp smoked paprika
- 2 tsp ground oregano
- 1 tsp chilli powder

Nutrition Information

Calories 391, Fat 0 g, Saturates 12 g, Sugar 12 g, Sodium 393 mg, Protein 43 g, Carbs 18 g, Fibre 2 g

Air Fryer Piri Piri Chicken Legs

Prep Time: 5 minutes
Cooking Time: 22 minutes
Additional Time: 30 minutes
Total Time: 57 minutes
Servings: 4
Difficulty: Show off

INGREDIENTS

- 4 chicken legs
- 2 tsp Piri Piri spice mix
- 120 g Piri Piri marinade sauce

DIRECTIONS

1. Add the Piri Piri spice mix and sauce to the uncooked chicken legs. Leave them in a bowl to marinade for approximately 30 minutes.
2. Transfer the chicken legs to the air fryer basket and cook at 190 °C/380 °F for 22 minutes, turning the chicken legs over at the halfway point.
3. Check that the chicken legs are ready. The juice running clear or an internal temperature of 75 °C/165 °F is a good indicator that they are thoroughly cooked.

Nutrition Information

Calories 359, Fat 27 g, Saturates 7 g, Sugar 3 g, Protein 24 g, Carbs 4 g, Fibre 1 g

Air Fryer Chicken Nuggets

Prep Time: 10 minutes
Cooking Time: 8 minutes
Total Time: 18 minutes
Servings: 4
Difficulty: Not too tricky

INGREDIENTS

- 3-4 chicken breasts
- 2 eggs, beaten
- 100 g breadcrumbs
- Seasoning of your choice (paprika, salt, garlic powder, and pepper are especially delicious).

DIRECTIONS

1. Cut the chicken breasts into small, chicken nugget-sized chunks.
2. Set up your breading station using two bowls for beaten eggs and your seasoning breadcrumb mix.
3. Using kitchen tongs or your fingers, dip each piece of chicken into the beaten egg and then into the seasoned breadcrumbs.
4. Place the chicken nuggets in the air fryer basket. You may need to cook these nuggets in separate batches, depending on the size of your air fryer.
5. Cook the chicken nuggets at 200 °C/400 °F for 8-10 minutes, flipping them over at the halfway mark.

Nutrition Information

Calories 340, Fat 8 g, Saturates 2 g, Sugar 2 g, Sodium 549 mg, Protein 44 g, Carbs 20g, Fibre 2 g

Air Fryer Chicken Kyiv Balls

Prep Time: 15 minutes
Cooking Time: 10 minutes
Total Time: 25 minutes
Servings: 2
Difficulty: Show off

INGREDIENTS

- 300 g ground chicken
- 3 cloves of garlic, crushed
- 100 g breadcrumbs
- 120 g butter
- 2 fresh parsley sprigs, leaves chopped
- 1 egg

DIRECTIONS

1. Mix together the butter, chopped parsley, and crushed garlic.
2. Divide the butter into 12 equal-sized balls. Pop them into the fridge or freezer to harden up.
3. Once the garlic butter balls have hardened up a bit, you will wrap the ground chicken around them. Take a little bit of ground chicken at a time and wrap it around the butter ball in a thin layer.
4. Beat the egg in a bowl and set aside a second bowl with breadcrumbs. You can also season your breadcrumbs with your favourite spices, like paprika, salt, and pepper.
5. Using kitchen tongs, dip the balls in the egg mixture, ensuring that it is properly coated, followed by the seasoned breadcrumbs. Use your hands to firmly secure the breadcrumbs on the kiev balls.
6. Spray the balls with a little bit of cooking oil, and place them in the air fryer basket for 10 minutes at 200 °C/400 °F. Turn them over at the halfway mark.

Nutrition Information

Calories 154, Fat 9 g, Saturates 5 g, Sugar 0 g, Sodium 280 mg, Protein 13 g, Carbs 7 g, Fibre 0 g

Air Fryer Nando's Style Chicken Breasts

Prep Time: 5 minutes
Cooking Time: 18 minutes
Total Time: 23 minutes
Servings: 4
Difficulty: Not too tricky

INGREDIENTS

- 500 g chicken breast
- 1 sachet of Nando's peri peri hot rub
- 1 tbsp tomato puree
- 1 tbsp olive oil

DIRECTIONS

1. Mix the tomato puree, Nando's peri rub, and olive oil in a bowl until it becomes a paste.
2. Add the chicken breasts into the bowl and spread the marinade over them, flipping them over to coat both sides.
3. Place the marinated chicken breasts into the air fryer basket and be sure that they are spread in an even, single layer.
4. Cook at 200 °C/400 °F for 16-18 minutes, checking periodically. You will also want to flip the chicken breasts over halfway through the cooking time.
5. Remove the cooked chicken breasts from the air fryer and let them rest for a few minutes before slicing or serving.

Nutrition Information

Calories 238, Fat 8 g, Saturates 2 g, Sugar 0 g, Sodium 94 mg, Protein 39 g, Carbs 0 g, Fibre 0 g

Air Fryer Chicken Tikka Masala

Prep Time: 20 minutes
Cooking Time: 8 minutes
Additional Time: 1 hour
Total Time: 1 hour 28 minutes
Servings: 4
Difficulty: Not too tricky

INGREDIENTS

- 3 boneless, skinless chicken breasts
- 1 packet chicken tikka masala sauce

DIRECTIONS

1. Dice your chicken into 2 cm pieces.
2. Mix together the chicken pieces and tikka masala sauce. Let it rest, covered, for 30 minutes so that the chicken can marinate with all of the delicious tikka masala flavours.
3. Place your chicken pieces into the air fryer tray. Let the chicken cook for 5-10 minutes on 175 °C/350 °F heat.
4. After your timer has run out, make sure that the chicken is thoroughly cooked by referencing your meat thermometer.

Nutrition Information

Calories 216, Fat 8 g, Saturates 3 g,
Sugar 3 g, Sodium 328 mg, Protein 29 g,
Carbs 5 g, Fibre 1 g

Air Fryer Turkey Crown

Prep Time: 5 minutes
Cooking Time: 50 minutes
Total Time: 55 minutes
Servings: 6
Difficulty: Show off

INGREDIENTS

- 1.7 kg turkey crown
- 1 tsp vegetable oil
- 1 tsp dried mixed herbs
- 1 clementine, halved
- 1 shallot, halved
- 2 garlic cloves, halved
- A few fresh herb sprigs

DIRECTIONS

1. Preheat the air fryer temperature to 180 °C/360 °F.
2. Pat, the turkey crown dry with a clean kitchen towel, then rub the whole thing down with oil. Season the crown well, then scatter the dried herbs all over the skin. If possible, stuff the clementine, shallot, garlic cloves, and fresh herb sprigs into the cavity. If this isn't possible, you can tuck them around the turkey crown once it is placed inside the air fryer basket.
3. Place the turkey crown into the air fryer basket skin-side down.
4. Cook the turkey for 30 minutes, then turn the crown over and cook for an additional 20-30 minutes. By the end of the cooking time, the meat thermometer should

Nutrition Information

Calories 424, Fat 17 g, Saturates 5 g,
Sugar 10 g, Sodium 1 g, Protein 57 g,
Carbs 11 g, Fibre 2 g

Air Fryer Balsamic Chicken and Vegetables

Prep Time: 5 minutes
Cooking Time: 17 minutes
Total Time: 22 minutes
Servings: 4
Difficulty: Show off

INGREDIENTS

Chicken and Vegetables
- 1 large chicken breast
- 10 cherry tomatoes
- 1 small zucchini
- 1 bell pepper

Balsamic Glaze
- 1 tbsp balsamic vinegar
- 1 tbsp honey
- 1 tbsp olive oil
- 1 tsp oregano
- 1 tsp basil
- 1 tsp garlic puree
- Salt, to taste
- Pepper, to taste

DIRECTIONS

1. Half the cherry tomatoes and cut the bell pepper into bite-sized chunks. Cut the zucchini into slices, then quarters, and the chicken into chunks as well.
2. Mix all of the balsamic ingredients into a bowl and mix. If the balsamic glaze is too thin, you can add more honey. If the glaze is too thick, you can add more balsamic vinegar.
3. Toss the chicken and vegetables in the balsamic glaze until well-coated.
4. Place the chicken and vegetables together in the air fryer for 12 minutes at 180 °C/360 °F. Stir the chicken and vegetables once the timer goes off, then cook for a final 5 minutes at 200 °C/400 °F.

Nutrition Information

Calories 143, Fat 5 g, Saturates 1 g, Sugar 8 g, Sodium 77 mg, Protein 13 g, Carbs 11 g

Zesty Italian Chicken Drumsticks

Prep Time: 10 minutes
Cooking Time: 30 minutes
Optional Additional Time: 30 minutes
Optional Total Time: 1 hour 10 minutes
Servings: 3
Difficulty: Not too tricky

INGREDIENTS

- 6 chicken drumsticks
- 6 tbsp olive oil
- 1 tbsp white wine vinegar
- 2 tsp garlic puree
- 1 tsp dark brown sugar
- Juice from ½ a lemon
- Zest from 1 lemon
- Basil, chopped

DIRECTIONS

1. Place marinade ingredients into a bag, seal, and use your fingers to mix the ingredients together.
2. Add the chicken drumsticks to the bag, mix together with the marinade, and leave the marinade to sit for 30 minutes or so. You can cook straight away if you are low on time.
3. Preheat the air fryer temperature to 190°C/380 °F.
4. Place the marinated chicken drumsticks in a single layer in the air fryer basket, and cook for 25 minutes. Flip the drumsticks over at the halfway point of cook time.

Nutrition Information

Calories 502, Fat 42 g, Saturates 8 g, Sugar 1 g, Sodium 160 mg, Protein 27 g, Carbs 3 g, Fibre 1 g

Tandoori Chicken Tikka Kebab

Prep Time: 10 minutes
Cooking Time: 15 minutes
Optional Additional Time: up to 2 hours
Optional Total Time: 2 hours 25 minutes
Servings: 6
Difficulty: Not too tricky

INGREDIENTS

- 2-3 large chicken breasts, cubed
- 4 tbsp yoghourt
- 2 tbsp tandoori masala spice blend powder
- 2 cloves garlic, crushed
- 1 lemon, ½ for juice, ½ sliced into wedges for serving
- Spray oil

DIRECTIONS

1. Soak the skewers in water while you are preparing the chicken, then cut them down to size in order to fit in the air fryer basket.
2. In a bowl, mix the yoghurt, tandoori masala, garlic, and lemon juice.
3. Add the cubed chicken to the bowl with the sauce and stir to coat. You can then leave the chicken to marinade for up to 2 hours in the fridge.
4. Thread the chicken on the kebab skewers; expect 4-6 kebabs full of chicken.
5. Preheat the air fryer to 180 °C/360 °F, then add the chicken skewers to the air fryer basket, spray them with oil, and cook for 15 minutes.

Nutrition Information

Calories 107, Fat 2 g, Saturates 1 g, Sugar 1 g, Sodium 98 mg, Protein 17 g, Carbs 4 g, Fibre 1 g

Stuffed Turkey Breast

Prep Time: 15 minutes
Cooking Time: 20 minutes
Additional Time: 10 minutes
Total Time: 45 minutes
Servings: 8
Difficulty: Show off

INGREDIENTS

- 4 cloves garlic, pressed
- 1 large shallot, finely chopped
- 1 c flat-leaf parsley, chopped
- 2 tbsp fresh rosemary, finely chopped
- 1 tbsp grated orange zest
- 4 tbsp olive oil, divided
- Kosher salt
- 2 skin-on boneless turkey breast halves, about 1 kg total

DIRECTIONS

1. Heat the air fryer to 190 °C/380 °F.
2. In a medium bowl, mix the garlic, shallot, chopped parsley, chopped rosemary, orange zest, 2 tbsp olive oil, and ½ tsp salt and pepper each.
3. Remove the skin from each turkey breast in one piece, carefully handling as not to tear it, and set it aside.
4. Butterfly and pound each breast to ½ cm thick. Divide the herb mixture on top of each breast, leaving a 1 cm border all the way around. Roll each turkey breast starting at the short end. Place the skin back on top of each breast, tucking it under the edges, then tie it with a kitchen string.
5. Brush each turkey breast with 1 tbsp oil and season with ¼ tsp salt.
6. Air fry the turkey breasts until they are cooked through, about 20 minutes.
7. Remove the turkey from the air fryer, then let it rest for 10 minutes.

Nutrition Information

Calories 183, Fat 16 g, Saturates 6 g, Sugar 1 g, Sodium 432 mg, Protein 2 g, Carbs 8 g, Fibre 2 g

Tandoori Spiced
Cauliflower Chicken Flatbreads

Prep Time: 11 minutes
Cooking Time: 29 minutes
Total Time: 40 minutes
Servings: 4
Difficulty: Show off

INGREDIENTS

- 1 small red onion, thinly sliced
- 1 ½ tsp paprika
- 1 ½ tsp coriander
- 1 ½ tsp ground cumin
- 2 tsp smoked paprika
- ¼ tsp cayenne pepper
- ¼ tsp dry mustard powder
- ⅛ tsp ground cardamom
- Kosher salt
- 3 tbsp olive oil
- 1 tbsp tomato paste
- 2 cloves garlic, grated
- 2 tsp fresh ginger, grated
- 0.75 kg cauliflower, trimmed and cut into florets
- 0.5 kg chicken breast, cut into 4 cm cubes
- 1 small yellow onion, cut into wedges
- 1 tbsp fresh lemon juice
- 4 pieces naan bread, warmed
- ½ c Greek yoghourt

DIRECTIONS

1. Place red onion in a bowl, cover with cold water, and let it sit.
2. In a large bowl, combine the paprika, coriander, cumin, smoked paprika, cayenne, mustard powder, cardamom, and 1 tsp salt. Add in the oil, tomato paste, garlic, and ginger.
3. Add the cauliflower and toss to coat. Add the chicken and toss it together. Let the chicken and cauliflower sit for 15 minutes.
4. Heat the air fryer to 190°C/380 °F.
5. Remove the chicken from the bowl, and place it in a second bowl with the yellow onion wedges.
6. Air fry the cauliflower in a single layer in the air fryer basket for 14 minutes, shaking the basket halfway through until slightly browned. Place the cauliflower on a plate.
7. Air fry the chicken for 8 minutes or until cooked through.
8. While the chicken is cooking, drain the red onion and toss it in some lemon juice and ¼ tsp salt.
9. Spread the naan with yoghurt, top with the chicken and vegetables, then sprinkle onion and cilantro on top.

Nutrition Information

Calories 510, Fat 18 g, Saturates 3 g,
Sodium 919 mg, Protein 30 g,
Carbs 55 g, Fibre 5 g

Italian Marinated Chicken

Prep Time: 17 minutes
Cooking Time: 13 minutes
Additional Time: 10 minutes
Total Time: 40 minutes
Servings: 4
Difficulty: Not too tricky

INGREDIENTS

- 3 tbsp white wine vinegar
- 2 tbsp red wine vinegar
- 2 cloves garlic
- 2 tsp Dijon mustard
- 1 tsp agave or honey
- 6 fresh basil leaves
- ½ tbsp fresh thyme leaves
- 2/3 c olive oil
- ½ tsp red pepper flakes
- ¼ tsp dried oregano
- 4 6-oz chicken breasts
- 2 peppers, thinly sliced
- 1 c cherry tomatoes, halved
- ½ small red onion, thinly sliced
- 12 c mixed salad greens
- 1 oz parmesan, shaved

DIRECTIONS

1. In a blender, combine the vinegar, garlic, mustard, agave, basil, thyme, and ½ tsp salt and pepper each. Blend until smooth. Add the oil and blend the marinade again to mix but not emulsify for about 10 seconds. Stir in the red pepper flakes and oregano.
2. Coat the chicken with 1/3 cup of the dressing, and set aside to marinate for 10 minutes at room temperature to overnight in the fridge.
3. Heat the air fryer to 200 °C/400 °F.
4. Add the marinated chicken to the air fryer basket and cook for 4 minutes. Using tongs, flip the chicken and cook for an additional 8-9 minutes until the chicken is golden brown and cooked through.

Nutrition Information

Calories 424, Fat 25 g, Saturates 5 g,
Sodium 526 mg, Protein 39 g,
Carbs 14 g, Fibre 3 g

Air Fryer Chicken Parmesan

Prep Time: 10 minutes
Cooking Time: 40 minutes
Total Time: 50 minutes
Servings: 4
Difficulty: Not too tricky

INGREDIENTS

- 2 large chicken breasts
- Kosher salt, to taste
- Pepper, to taste
- 1/3 c all-purpose flour
- 2 large eggs
- 1 c breadcrumbs
- ¼ c freshly grated parmesan
- 1 tsp dried oregano
- ½ crushed red pepper flakes
- ½ tsp garlic powder
- 1 c marinara sauce
- 1 c shredded mozzarella

DIRECTIONS

1. Butterfly the chicken, creating 4 thin pieces of chicken. Season both sides with salt and pepper.
2. Place the flour in a shallow bowl and season with a large pinch of salt and pepper. In another shallow bowl, quickly beat the eggs to blend. In a third shallow bowl, combine the breadcrumbs, parmesan, and seasonings.
3. Coat the chicken in flour, then dip the breasts into the eggs. Let the excess drip off of the chicken, then dip the chicken into the breadcrumbs. Gently press to adhere the breadcrumbs to the chicken.
4. Arrange the chicken in the air fryer basket in an evenly-spaced single layer and set the temperature to 200 °C/400 °F. Cook the chicken for 5 minutes on each side, and top with the marinara sauce and shredded mozzarella. Cook for an additional 3 minutes, until the cheese is melted and golden in colour.

Nutrition Information

Calories 541, Fat 18 g, Saturates 8 g,
Sugar 5 g, Sodium 1530 mg, Protein 47 g,
Carbs 43 g, Fibre 3 g

This page is for your notes

CHAPTER 5

BEEF, PORK AND LAMB RECIPES

Air Fryer Beef Wellington

Prep Time: 40 minutes
Cooking Time: 40 minutes
Total Time: 1 hour 20 minutes
Servings: 2
Difficulty: Show off

INGREDIENTS

- 1 tbsp olive oil
- 2 x 150 g beef eye fillet steak
- 200 g button mushrooms, finely chopped
- 2 French shallots, peeled and finely chopped
- 2 garlic cloves, crushed
- 7 slices prosciutto
- 2 tsp Dijon mustard
- 1 sheet frozen puff pastry, freshly thawed
- 1 egg, lightly whisked
- Steamed broccolini to serve

DIRECTIONS

1. Heat the olive oil in a large frying pan over high heat. Cook the steaks for 3-4 minutes or until just browned on all sides. Transfer the browned steaks to a plate and let them cool slightly.
2. Reduce the pan heat to medium, and add mushrooms, shallots, and garlic to the pan. Cook them together for about 15 minutes or until a lot of the liquid has evaporated. The vegetables also need to cool slightly, so set them aside for 5 minutes or so.
3. Lay six of the prosciutto slices on a sheet of plastic wrap, overlapping slightly, to make a rectangle. Spread the mushy mixture over the prosciutto, leaving a thin border vacant. Place the steaks lengthwise on top of the vegetable mix. Fold the prosciutto over the steak slices, and lay the remaining prosciutto slice over the steaks to cover any of the gaps.
4. Place the beef Wellington in the fridge after wrapping firmly in plastic wrap for 20 minutes.
5. Lay the pastry on a flat surface, and unwrap the log. Place the log in the centre of the puff pastry. Fold the pastry over the beef Wellington log, and tuck the ends to seal it. Place the seam side down on a sheet of baking paper, and brush the top with egg wash. You can also score the pastry dough diagonally with a knife.
6. Place the log in the air fryer basket, and cook at 180 °C/360 °F for 20 minutes. This will give you a rare medium finish, so if you prefer your beef Wellington to be a bit more cooked-through, leave it in a bit longer.
7. Serve with broccolini and onion relish.

Nutrition Information

Calories 1073, Fat 70.2 g, Saturates 26.7 g,
Sugar 7.8 g, Sodium 1.7 mg, Protein 56.8 g,
Carbs 56.9 g, Fibre 4.9 g

Haggis, Neeps & Tatties

Prep Time: 15 minutes
Cooking Time: 1 hour 5 minutes
Total Time: 1 hour 20 minutes
Servings: 5
Difficulty: Show off

INGREDIENTS

Haggis
- 500 g haggis
- Salt, to taste
- Pepper, to taste

Neeps
- 1 kg neeps - swede/rutabaga
- 3 tbsp butter
- Salt, to taste
- Pepper, to taste
- Cream or milk, optional

Tatties
- 1.2 kg tatties - potatoes
- 125 mL milk
- 125 mL single cream
- 40 g butter
- Salt, to taste
- Pepper, to taste

DIRECTIONS

Haggis
1. Preheat your air fryer temperature to 180 °C/360 °F.
2. Wrap the haggis in a layer of tin foil and add to a lidded ovenproof dish with a thin layer of water.
3. Place the ovenproof dish in the air fryer basket, and cook for 1 hour. Check periodically to make sure that the water hasn't dried out.

Neeps
4. Dice the neeps into 2 cm cubes.
5. Gently boil the neeps in salt water for 20 minutes.
6. Drain the neeps in a colander and set out to air dry.
7. In a pan over low heat, place the butter and a splash of cream or milk (optional). Heat on low until the butter has melted.
8. Add the cooked swede into the pot, and mash to your desired consistency.

Tatties
9. Chop the potatoes into large, evenly sized-chunks.
10. Add the chopped potatoes to a deep pot and top with cold water. Add salt and gently boil on medium-high heat for 15-20 minutes.
11. When soft, drain the potatoes and leave them in the colander to dry.
12. Add cream, milk, and butter to a pot and heat it on low until the butter has melted. Turn off the stovetop heat, and add the potatoes back into the pot. Mash the ingredients together with a potato masher until the mixture has reached its desired consistency.

Nutrition Information

Calories 806, Fat 64 g, Saturates 36 g,
Sugar 11 g, Sodium 391 mg, Protein 18 g,
Carbs 37 g, Fibre 5 g

Air Fryer Cornish Pasties

Prep Time: 5 minutes
Cooking Time: 8 minutes
Total Time: 13 minutes
Servings: 3
Difficulty: Not too tricky

INGREDIENTS

- 200 g pre-cooked steak, chopped
- 500 g pie crust
- Egg wash
- 1 tsp mixed herbs
- Salt
- Pepper

DIRECTIONS

1. Place the pre-cooked steak in a bowl, ensuring that it is drained of liquid. You can use leftover beef stew or sirloin steak. Whatever you have in the fridge, really. Add salt, pepper, and mixed herbs to the steak and mix.
2. Roll out the pastry and cut out three smaller pastry circles with a pasty maker. Once cut, place the pastry circles on a clean, floured worktop.
3. One at a time, place the pasty circles on the pasty maker and load up the steak filling in the centre of each pastry, being mindful not to overfill it.
4. Fold the pasty maker closed, and press down. Make sure that it leaves a beautiful pasty pattern on the outskirts of the pasty. Repeat this process until you have used up all of your dough and filling.
5. Place a layer of foil in the air fryer basket in order to cover the tops of the pasties with an egg wash.
6. Air fry the pasties for 8 minutes at a temperature of 200 °C/400 °F.

Nutrition Information

Calories 860, Fat 47 g, Saturates 15 g, Sugar 1 g, Sodium 719 mg, Protein 25 g, Carbs 81 g, Fibre 4 g

Air Fryer Crispy Chilli Beef

Prep Time: 15 minutes
Cooking Time: 15 minutes
Total Time: 30 minutes
Servings: 2
Difficulty: Easy

INGREDIENTS

- 250 g thin-cut minute steak, sliced into thin strips
- 4 tbsp rice wine vinegar or white wine vinegar
- 2 tbsp cornflour
- 2 tbsp vegetable oil
- 2 tbsp sweet chilli sauce
- 2 tbsp tomato ketchup
- 2 garlic cloves, crushed
- Ginger, thumb-sized, sliced into matchsticks
- 1 red chilli, thinly sliced
- 1 red pepper, chopped
- 4 spring onions, sliced
- 1 tbsp soy sauce

DIRECTIONS

1. Combine the above marinade ingredients in a bowl and toss the strips of steak to coat. Leave the steak to sit in the marinade for up to 24 hours in your fridge.
2. Sprinkle the cornflour over the marinated steak and mix. Pull the strips apart and arrange them on a plate. Drizzle each piece of steak with some oil.
3. Heat the air fryer to 220 °C/440 °F. Place the beef on the cooking rack or in the air fryer basket for 6 minutes, then flip the pieces over and cook them for an additional 4-6 minutes until crispy.
4. While the beef streak is cooking in the air fryer, heat 2 tbsp vegetable oil in a large pan or wok and add in the chilli, garlic, ginger, the white ends of the spring onion and pepper. Cook for only 2-3 minutes, until the pepper softens. Add the vinegar, soy sauce, and sweet chilli sauce, as well as the tomato ketchup, to the wok. Stir until bubbling occurs.
5. Place the beef into the wok and ensure that each piece has been coated in the sauce mixture.

Nutrition Information

Calories 440, Fat 19 g, Saturates 3 g, Sugar 20 g, Sodium 3 g, Protein 31 g, Carbs 34 g, Fibre 3 g

Air Fryer Lamb Kofta Kebabs

Prep Time: 5 minutes
Cooking Time: 16 minutes
Total Time: 21 minutes
Servings: 4
Difficulty: Not too tricky

INGREDIENTS

- 500 g ground minced lamb
- 1 tsp coriander
- 1 tsp mixed spice
- 1 tsp chilli flakes
- 1 tsp turmeric
- 1 tsp cumin
- 1 tsp mixed herbs
- ½ tsp tandoori seasoning

DIRECTIONS

1. Load all of the ingredients for the kofta into a mixing bowl, and mix well with your hands.
2. Form the meat into thick sausage shapes like a kebab.
3. Place the meat onto kebab skewers and place them directly in the air fryer basket. Make sure that they do not touch each other in order to ensure even cooking.
4. Cook the kebabs for 8 minutes in the air fryer at 180 °C/360 °F. Turn them over, then cook for an additional 8 minutes.

Nutrition Information

Calories 362, Fat 30 g, Saturates 13 g, Sugar 1 g, Sodium 83 mg, Protein 21 g, Carbs 1 g, Fibre 1 g

Air Fryer Slimming World Burgers

Prep Time: 5 minutes
Cooking Time: 17 minutes
Total Time: 22 minutes
Servings: 2
Difficulty: Not too tricky

INGREDIENTS

- 250 g Slimming World Frozen Chips
- 450 g lean minced beef
- ½ small onion
- 2 tsp garlic puree
- 1 tbsp basil
- 1 tbsp oregano
- salt, to taste
- Vinegar, to taste
- Pepper, to taste
- Burger bun, optional
- Salad garnish, optional

DIRECTIONS

1. Peel and dice your onion, then load it into the mixing bowl with minced beef and the seasonings. Mix the patty mixture with your hands and form them into 2 burger patties.
2. Place the burger patties in the air fryer basket on one side and add the frozen chips to the other side. Air fry the burgers and chips for 12 minutes at 160 F/320 C.
3. When the air fryer timer has finished, remove the chips and place them in a bowl with salt and vinegar. Toss the chips in your salt-vinegar solution, then remove and place them back in the air fryer. Flip the burger patties over as well.
4. Air dry the burgers and chips for an additional 5 minutes at 200 C/400 F. Serve with a burger bun, your favourite condiments, and a salad garnish.

Nutrition Information

Calories 659, Fat 30 g, Saturates 11 g, Sugar 1 g, Sodium 764 mg, Protein 53 g, Carbs 44 g, Fibre 7 g

Air Fryer Sausage and Chips

Prep Time: 0 minutes
Cooking Time: 16 minutes
Total Time: 16 minutes
Servings: 4
Difficulty: Easy

INGREDIENTS

- 8 frozen sausages
- 750 g frozen chips

DIRECTIONS

1. Place the frozen chips in the air fryer basket and layer the sausages on top of them.
2. Cook the sausages and chips for 4 minutes at 200 °C/400 °F.
3. Shake the basket and cook for 8 minutes at the same temperature.
4. Shake the basket once more and cook for the final 4 minutes at the same temperature.

Nutrition Information

Calories 2349, Fat 176 g, Saturates 57 g, Sodium 4712 mg, Protein 79 g, Carbs 113 g, Fibre 17 g

Air Fryer Steak and Chips

Prep Time: 6 minutes
Cooking Time: 22 minutes
Total Time: 28 minutes
Servings: 2
Difficulty: Not too tricky

INGREDIENTS

- 2 rump steaks
- 500 g white potatoes
- 1 tsp olive oil
- 2 tsp garlic butter
- Salt, to taste
- Pepper, to taste

DIRECTIONS

1. Peel and chop your potatoes into french fry-style chips. Place them in a mixing bowl, then season with salt and pepper. Drizzle the potatoes with a dash of olive oil, and mix them with your hands, coating the potatoes evenly.
2. Place the chips in the air fryer for 10 minutes at 160 °C/320 °F.
3. Pound the steaks with a tenderiser, then season them with salt and pepper.
4. When the air fryer timer goes off, shake the basket of chips and place the steaks on top. Cook for an additional 6 minutes at the same temperature.
5. Flip the steaks over in the basket, then cook for 6 more minutes at the same temperature.
6. Spread a nice layer of garlic butter over the steaks before serving.

Nutrition Information

Calories 716, Fat 38 g, Saturates 17 g., Sugar 2 g, Sodium 168 mg, Protein 51 g, Carbs 44 g, Fibre 6 g

Air Fryer Leg of Lamb

Prep Time: 5 minutes
Cooking Time: 1 hour
Total Time: 1 hour 5 minutes
Servings: 4
Difficulty: Show off

INGREDIENTS

- 1.4 kg leg of lamb
- Air fryer roast potatoes
- Salt, to taste
- Pepper, to taste

DIRECTIONS

1. Season the leg of lamb with salt and pepper, then place it on the top shelf of your air fryer oven.
2. Cook the lamb leg for 20 minutes at 180 °C/360 °F.
3. While the lamb starts cooking, you can prepare your roast potatoes by peeling, chopping, and seasoning them to your liking.
4. Remove some of the lamb leg juices from the air fryer tray when your timer goes off, and toss the potatoes in the juices to coat. Place your potatoes on the second rack.
5. Cook the lamb and potatoes for an additional 40 minutes at the same temperature as before, before serving.

Nutrition Information

Calories 640, Fat 23 g, Saturates 8 g, Sodium 310 mg, Protein 103 g

Suya Beef Kebabs

Prep Time: 13 minutes
Cooking Time: 12 minutes
Total Time: 25 minutes
Servings: 6
Difficulty: Not too tricky

INGREDIENTS

- 450 g sirloin steak
- 1 cube chicken stock
- 2 tbsp groundnut oil
- ¼ tsp garlic powder
- 4 tbsp suya seasoning

DIRECTIONS

1. Use a meat tenderiser to flatten the steaks, then slice the thin steaks into strips.
2. Thread the steak onto the kebab sticks.
3. Brush the oil onto the steak.
4. Make the suya seasoning by adding the garlic powder and chicken stock cube to your preexisting suya seasoning. Spread the seasoning across a large plate, then coat the beef in the seasoning.
5. Preheat your air fryer to 200 °C/400 °F, place the kebabs in the air fryer basket, and cook for 5-6 minutes.

Nutrition Information

Calories 127, Fat 6 g, Saturates 2 g, Sugar 0 g, Sodium 153 mg, Protein 13 g, Carbs 5 g, Fibre 3 g

Lemony Garlic and Herb Pork Tenderloin

Prep Time: 12 minutes
Cooking Time: 18 minutes
Additional Time: 10 minutes
Total Time: 40 minutes
Servings: 4
Difficulty: Not too tricky

INGREDIENTS

- ¼ c finely chopped mixed fresh herbs (parsley, mint, thyme, rosemary, etc.)
- 1 clove garlic, finely grated
- 1 tsp grated lemon zest
- ¼ tsp red pepper flakes
- ¼ c + 1 tbsp olive oil
- 0.5 kg pork tenderloin
- Kosher salt

DIRECTIONS

1. Heat the air fryer to a temperature of 200 °C/400 °F.
2. In a small bowl, combine the above herbs, garlic, lemon zest, red pepper flakes, and ¼ c olive oil. Set aside.
3. Season the pork with 1 tsp salt and add to the air fryer basket for 7 minutes.
4. Brush the pork with the herb-oil mixture, then air fry for an additional 8-11 minutes until fully cooked. Transfer the pork to the cutting board and let rest for 10 minutes before slicing and serving.

Nutrition Information

Calories 415, Fat 29 g, Saturates 8 g,
Sugar 1 g, Sodium 750mg, Protein 32 g,
Carbs 7 g, Fibre 1 g

Marinated Flank Steak

Prep Time: 5 minutes
Cooking Time: 10 minutes
Additional Time: 2 hours 10 minutes
Total Time: 2 hours 25 minutes
Servings: 4-6
Difficulty: Show off

INGREDIENTS

Marinade
- 1 1/2 tbsp grated orange zest
- 1/3 c orange juice
- 1 tbsp grated lime zest
- 2 tbsp lime juice
- 2 tbsp olive oil
- 1 ½ tsp cumin seeds
- 2 cloves garlic, finely chopped

Flank Steak
- 1 0.75-1 kg flank steak
- Kosher salt

DIRECTIONS

1. Combine all marinade ingredients into a plastic bag, pressing around to mix together. Add steak and seal, turning to coat. Let the marinade sit for anywhere from 30 minutes to 2 hours.
2. Heat the air fryer to 200 °C/400 °F. Remove the steak from the marinade, scraping off any chunks of citrus zest. Season with salt and pepper, then add to the air fryer basket.
3. Air fry the steak for 8-10 minutes for a medium rare steak. This will depend on the thickness of the steak.
4. Let the steak rest for approximately 10 minutes before slicing and serving.

Nutrition Information

Calories 220, Fat 11 g, Saturates 4 g,
Sugar 5 g, Sodium 245 mg, Protein 28 g,
Carbs 1 g, Fibre 0 g

Air Fryer Meatball Sub

Prep Time: 19 minutes
Cooking Time: 11 minutes
Total Time: 30 minutes
Servings: 4
Difficulty: Not too tricky

INGREDIENTS

- 2 large eggs
- 2 tsp balsamic vinegar
- Kosher salt, to taste
- Pepper, to taste
- 1/3 c breadcrumbs
- 4 cloves garlic, 2 grated and 2 chopped
- ¼ c parmesan cheese
- ½ c flat leaf parsley chopped
- 227 g sweet Italian sausage, casings removed
- 227 g ground beef
- 0.5 kg cherry tomatoes
- 1 red chile, sliced
- 1 tbsp olive oil
- 4 small hero rolls, toasted and split
- 6 tbsp ricotta cheese
- Basil, for serving

DIRECTIONS

1. In a large bowl, whisk the eggs, vinegar, and ½ tsp of salt and pepper. Add the breadcrumbs, then let sit for 1 minute. Stir in the grated garlic and parmesan, followed by the parsley. Add sausage and beef to the mix, then gently mix.
2. Shape the meat into 20 balls, then place the balls in a single layer in the air fryer basket. Air fry the meatballs for 5 minutes at 200 °C/400 °F.
3. In a bowl, toss the chile, chopped garlic, and tomatoes with oil and ¼ tsp each of salt and pepper. Scatter the mixture over the meatballs and continue air frying until the meatballs are fully cooked, 5-6 minutes.
4. Spread the ricotta over the toasted rolls, then top them with meatballs, grated parmesan, and roasted tomatoes and chile. Garnish with basil if desired.

Nutrition Information

*Calories 594, Fat 34 g, Saturates 14 g,
Sugar 9 g, Sodium 1895 mg, Protein 36 g,
Carbs 35 g, Fibre 3 g*

Air Fryer Cheeseburger Nachos

Prep Time: 10 minutes
Cooking Time: 15 minutes
Total Time: 25 minutes
Servings: 4
Difficulty: Not too tricky

INGREDIENTS

- 1 tsp vegetable oil
- ½ onion, finely chopped
- 300 g 5%fat steak mince
- ½ tsp smoked paprika
- ½ tsp chilli powder, optional
- 1 tbsp tomato puree
- 75 g cheese, grated
- 75 g mozzarella, grated
- 200 g lightly salted tortilla chips
- 3 tbsp mayonnaise
- 1 tsp American yellow mustard
- 1 tbsp ketchup
- dash of Worcestershire sauce
- 50 g sliced gherkins
- 1 salad tomato, chopped

DIRECTIONS

1. Preheat the air fryer temperature to 200 °C/400 °F. Line the air fryer with a sheet of aluminium foil, then place the onion and mince in the basket. Cook for 5 minutes, stirring once. Make sure that the meat is fully browned.
2. Add the smoked paprika and chilli powder, followed by tomato puree, salt, and pepper. Cook for an additional 2 minutes. Remove the minced mixture and set it aside.
3. Mix together the shredded cheeses.
4. Add ½ the tortilla chips to the air fryer basket, then sprinkle ½ of the cheese on top. Heap some of the mince to the centre, and cover the rest of the basket with tortilla chips. Add the rest of the mince and cheese on top, then cook for 3-5 minutes.
5. While the nachos cook, mix the mayonnaise, ketchup, and mustard together in a bowl. Season the sauce with salt, pepper, a dash of Worcestershire sauce, and 1 tbsp pickle juice.
6. When the nachos are done, top them with the diced tomato, gherkins, and remaining onion. Drizzle the sauce on top before serving.

Nutrition Information

*Calories 580, Fat 35 g, Saturates 10 g,
Sugar 4 g, Sodium 2 g, Protein 28 g,
Carbs 37 g, Fibre 3 g*

Air Fryer Meatballs

Prep Time: 10 minutes
Cooking Time: 7 minutes
Additional Time: 6 minutes
Total Time: 23 minutes
Servings: 16 meatballs
Difficulty: Not too tricky

INGREDIENTS

- 500 g beef mince
- 1 clove garlic, crushed
- 1 tsp dried mixed herbs
- 1 egg
- 1 tbsp breadcrumbs, optional

DIRECTIONS

1. Mix all of the meatball ingredients together until they are well combined.
2. Using your hands, form small, round balls. This recipe makes about 16 meatballs.
3. Place the meatballs in the air fryer at 180 °C/350 °F for 7 minutes. Check on them at the halfway point and flip them over if necessary.
4. If you want to add sauce, transfer the meatballs to an ovenproof dish and add the tomato sauce on top. Cook them in the sauce in the air fryer for an additional 6-8 minutes.

Nutrition Information

Calories 2679, Fat 11 g, Saturates 5 g, Sugar 0 g, Sodium 137 mg, Protein 38 g, Carbs 2 g, Fibre 0 g

Air Fryer Pizza Rolls

Prep Time: 10 minutes
Cooking Time: 8 minutes
Total Time: 18 minutes
Servings: 4
Difficulty: Not too tricky

INGREDIENTS

- 240 g Greek yoghourt
- 350 g self-raising flour
- 1 tin pizza sauce
- Grated cheese
- 1 tsp dried herbs, optional
- Pizza toppings of your choice

DIRECTIONS

1. Mix the flour and yoghurt together in a bowl until a dough is formed. You can add more flour if the dough is too sticky or water if the dough is too dry. You will need to be able to roll the dough without it sticking to the pin or falling apart.
2. On a lightly floured work surface, roll out the dough into a rectangle.
3. Spread the pizza sauce across the dough, but make sure that your sauce isn't too runny.
4. Sprinkle the grated cheese overtop, followed by your favourite toppings.
5. Roll the pizza dough into a roll, lengthwise, until it forms a sausage shape.
6. Using a sharp or serrated knife, cut the log into even slices.
7. Place the pizza rolls in the bottom of the air fryer basket, and cook for 8 minutes at 180 °C/350 °F. Check on them halfway through the cooking time.

Nutrition Information

Calories 393, Fat 5 g, Saturates 2 g, Sugar 6 g, Sodium 1276 mg, Protein 14 g, Carbs 72 g, Fibre 3 g

Air Fryer Pork Bites

Prep Time: 10 minutes
Cooking Time: 6 minutes
Total Time: 16 minutes
Servings: 4
Difficulty: Easy

INGREDIENTS

- 0.5 kg pork tenderloin
- 2 tbsp olive oil
- 1 tbsp cajun seasoning

DIRECTIONS

1. Preheat the air fryer temperature to 200 °C/400 °F.
2. Cut the pork into bite-sized pieces and toss them with the oil and seasoning.
3. Place the pork bites in a single layer in the air fryer and cook for 5-6 minutes.

Nutrition Information

Calories 203, Fat 11 g, Saturates 2 g,
Sugar 1 g, Sodium 60 mg, Protein 24 g,
Carbs 1 g, Fibre 1 g

Air Fryer Lamb Chops

Prep Time: 5 minutes
Cooking Time: 8 minutes
Additional Time: 1 hour
Total Time: 1 hour 13 minutes
Servings: 4
Difficulty: Not too tricky

INGREDIENTS

- 75 kg lamb chops
- 2 tbsp olive oil
- 1 tbsp red wine vinegar
- 1 tsp dried rosemary
- ½ tsp dried oregano
- ½ tsp kosher salt
- ½ tsp garlic powder
- ¼ tsp black pepper

DIRECTIONS

1. Combine the lamb chops, olive oil, red wine vinegar, and seasoning. Rub the marinade into the meat and let it sit for 1 hour in the fridge.
2. Preheat the air fryer setting to 200 °C/400 °F.
3. Add the seasoned lamb chops to the air fryer basket and cook for 7-9 minutes, flipping the chops over halfway through the cooking time

Nutrition Information

Calories 350, Fat 19 g, Saturates 6 g,
Sugar 1 g, Sodium 391 mg, Protein 42 g,
Carbs 1 g, Fibre 1 g

Air Fryer Lamb Rack

Prep Time: 3 minutes
Cooking Time: 12 minutes
Additional Time: 5 minutes
Total Time: 20 minutes
Servings: 2
Difficulty: Show off

INGREDIENTS

- 2 racks lamb
- 2 tbsp dried rosemary
- 3 tbsp olive oil
- 1 tbsp dried thyme
- 1 ½ tsp dried garlic
- 1 tsp dried onion powder
- Salt, to taste
- Pepper, to taste

DIRECTIONS

1. Add the marinade ingredients together and stir to combine.
2. Remove the excess fat from the lamb racks and brush the lamb with the herb marinade seasoning.
3. Preheat the air fryer temperature to 190 °C/375 °F for 5 minutes before adding the lamb.
4. Place the meat on the grill rack (or air fryer basket lined with a sheet of parchment paper) in the air fryer meat-side down.
5. Cook the lamb for 12 minutes.
6. Remove the lamb racks from the air fryer and wrap it in foil, letting it rest 5-10 minutes before serving.

Nutrition Information

Calories 761, Fat 56 g, Saturates 25 g, Sugar 0 g, Sodium 318 mg, Protein 62 g, Carbs 3 g, Fibre 1 g

Air Fryer Mongolian Beef

Prep Time: 10 minutes
Cooking Time: 10 minutes
Total Time: 20 minutes
Servings: 2
Difficulty: Show off

INGREDIENTS

- 0.5 kg flank steak
- ¼ c cornstarch
- 2 tbsp olive oil
- 4 cloves minced garlic
- 1 tbsp minced ginger
- ½ c low sodium soy sauce
- ½ c water
- ½ c brown sugar
- 2 green onions, chopped

DIRECTIONS

1. Slice the flank steak into thin strips, cutting against the grain.
2. Add the cornstarch to the steak slices and toss to coat. Let the steak sit in the cornstarch for 5 minutes.
3. Preheat the air fryer temperature setting to 200 °C/400 °F.
4. Add the steak to the air fryer and spray it with oil generously.
5. Air fry for 8-10 minutes, shaking the basket every 2-3 minutes.
6. While the steak is cooking in the air fryer, heat the olive oil in a skillet on the stove, then add the garlic and ginger for 30 seconds.
7. Add the soy sauce, water, and brown sugar. Stir well.
8. Bring the sauce to a boil and cook it for 6-7 minutes, until the sauce has thickened.
9. Add the cooked steak to the sauce and cook for an additional 1-2 minutes.
10. Sprinkle with chopped green onion before serving.

Nutrition Information

Calories 423, Fat 16 g, Saturates 4 g, Sugar 23 g, Sodium 1221 mg, Protein 35 g, Carbs 33 g, Fibre 1 g

This page is for your notes

CHAPTER 6

VEGAN AND VEGETARIAN RECIPES

Scottish Oatcakes (Vegetarian)

Prep Time: 10 minutes
Cooking Time: 15 minutes
Total Time: 25 minutes
Servings: 12
Difficulty: Not too tricky

INGREDIENTS

- 225 g medium oatmeal
- 60 g wholemeal flour
- ½ tsp salt
- ½ tsp sugar
- ½ tsp bicarbonate of soda
- 60 g butter
- Boiling water

DIRECTIONS

1. Mix 225 g oatmeal and 60 g wholemeal flour together in a bowl.
2. Add ½ tsp salt, ½ tsp sugar, and ½ tsp bicarbonate of soda to the dry ingredients in the bowl and mix well.
3. Cut 60 g butter into small cubes and add them to the oatmeal mixture.
4. Rub the butter cubes into the dry ingredients until you reach a breadcrumb consistency.
5. Boil a kettle of water and add enough water to make a stiff dough.
6. Sprinkle a little bit of flour onto your work surface or pastry mat and on your rolling pin. Roll out your oatmeal dough until it is ½ cm thick.
7. Cut the dough with 9 cm cookie cutter rounds. This will make about 12 oatcakes. If you wish to have more, use a smaller cutter.
8. For an oven-type air fryer, preheat the air fryer to 170 °C/340 °F. Lay the oatcakes on the tray of the air fryer and bake for 20 minutes.
9. For a top-opening/drawer air fryer, preheat the air fryer to 170 °C/340 °F. You will likely need to bake the oatcakes in batches, so place a sheet of baking paper at the bottom of the fryer basket and lay four oatcakes on top. Bake the oatcakes for 15 minutes.
10. Gently lift the oatcakes from the basket and leave them to cool before serving.

Nutrition Information

Calories 126, Fat 5 g, Saturates 3 g,
Sugar 0.2 g, Sodium 175 mg, Protein 4 g,
Carbs 16 g, Fibre 3 g

Air Fryer Buffalo Cauliflower Wings (Vegetarian)

Prep Time: 10 minutes
Cooking Time: 50 minutes
Total Time: 1 hour
Servings: 2-4
Difficulty: Not too tricky

INGREDIENTS

- 1 medium cauliflower (750 g), leaves removed and cut into florets
- 200 g buttermilk
- 100 g hot sauce
- 50 g plain flour
- 1 tbsp sweet smoked paprika
- 1 tbsp ground cumin
- 1 tbsp olive oil
- 1 tbsp honey
- ½ tbsp garlic powder

DIRECTIONS

1. Mix together the paprika, cumin, garlic powder, flour, and buttermilk with a generous pinch of salt and pepper into a bowl, making a smooth batter. Add the cauliflower florets, and coat them evenly.
2. Add the cauliflower florets to the air fryer basket in a single layer, shaking away any excess batter. You may need to cook the cauliflower in batches, depending on the size of the air fryer.
3. Cook the cauliflower for 18-20 minutes at 200 °C/400 °F, turning them over halfway through for even browning.
4. While the cauliflower is cooking, mix the hot sauce, honey, and olive oil in a large bowl. Gently mix the cooked cauliflower in the bowl and coat the florets in the hot sauce mixture. Return the cauliflower to the air fryer basket and cook for an additional 6-9 minutes until cooked through.

Nutrition Information

Calories 188, Fat 5 g, Saturates 1 g,
Sugar 11 g, Sodium 1 g, Protein 9 g,
Carbs 24 g, Fibre 5 g

Air Fryer Pasta Chips

Prep Time: 5 minutes
Cooking Time: 30 minutes
Total Time: 35 minutes
Servings: 46
Difficulty: Not too tricky

INGREDIENTS

- 7200 g pasta, we suggest farfalle
- 2 tbsp extra virgin olive oil
- 2 tsp smoked paprika
- 1 tsp ground cumin
- Dried oregano, 1 large pinch
- 1 tsp onion powder

DIRECTIONS

1. Cook the pasta following the bag/packet instructions, then drain and transfer the pasta to a large bowl.
2. Add the olive oil, spices, herbs, and some salt and pepper to the bowl and mix together until the pasta is well-coated.
3. Set the air fryer temperature to 180 °C/360 °F and cook the pasta for 15-20 minutes, shaking the basket every 5 minutes or so, until the pasta is golden and crisp.

Nutrition Information

Calories 144, Fat 4 g, Saturates 1 g,
Sugar 1 g, Sodium 1 g, Protein 4 g,
Carbs 21 g, Fibre 2 g

Air Fryer Tofu Popcorn Nuggets (Vegetarian)

Prep Time: 15 minutes
Cooking Time: 30 minutes
Additional Time: 30 minutes
Total Time: 1 hour 15 minutes
Servings: 24
Difficulty: Not too tricky

INGREDIENTS

- 1 block extra-firm tofu
- 4 tbsp plain flour
- 1 ½ tsp paprika
- 1 tsp Dijon mustard
- 125 mL milk
- 75 g Panko breadcrumbs
- ½ tsp garlic powder
- 1 tbsp bouillon powder

DIRECTIONS

1. Wrap the tofu in a clean kitchen towel, then place it on a large plate that has a lip around the edge of it. Put a heavy item like a frying pan, then add extra weight with cans or jars on top. Leave it like this for at least 30 minutes. The tofu should shrink and release any liquid.
2. Cut the tofu into 3 cm squares or rip it into the same-sized chunks. Add them to a bowl with 1 tbsp flour and 1 tsp paprika. Set this aside.
3. Place the remaining flour, dijon mustard, and milk in a medium bowl, and whisk the mixture until all of the lumps are broken up.
4. In a separate bowl, mix the breadcrumbs, garlic powder, bouillon powder, and ½ tsp paprika.
5. Heat the air fryer up to 190 °C/380 °F.
6. Dip each piece of tofu in the seasoned milk mixture, followed by the breadcrumbs mixture. Make sure that it is well coated before placing it on a plate or tray. Continue until all of the tofu is completely coated.
7. Lay the tofu pieces in a single layer on the bottom of the air fryer basket, and cook them for 12-15 minutes. You may have to cook these in batches. Set the batches aside until all of the tofu is cooked through.
8. Once all of the tofu is cooked, add it back into the air fryer and cook for an additional 2-3 minutes at 160 °C/320 °F.

Nutrition Information

Calories 44, Fat 1 g, Saturates 0 g, Sugar 1 g, Sodium 0 g, Protein 3 g, Carbs 5 g, Fibre 1 g

Air Fryer Carrot Chips (Vegetarian, Vegan Without Parmesan)

Prep Time: 5 minutes
Cooking Time: 15 minutes
Total Time: 20 minutes
Servings: 2
Difficulty: Not too tricky

INGREDIENTS

- 6 medium carrots
- 1.5 tsp extra virgin olive oil
- 2 tsp oregano
- 2 tsp thyme
- Salt, to taste
- Pepper, to taste
- 1 tbsp maple syrup (optional)
- 28 g parmesan cheese (optional)

DIRECTIONS

1. Peel and slice the carrots into chips/fries shapes and give them a wash.
2. Mix the carrots in a bowl with the extra virgin olive oil and seasoning.
3. Place the seasoned carrots in the air fryer basket and cook the carrots for 15 minutes at a temperature of 180 °C/360 °F. Check on them halfway through and shake the basket for even cooking.
4. Optional - toss the carrot chips in maple syrup and/or grated parmesan cheese for an extra kick of flavour.

Nutrition Information

Calories 190, Fat 7 g, Saturates 3 g, Sugar 15 g, Sodium 352 mg, Protein 7 g, Carbs 26 g, Fibre 6 g

Air Fryer Falafel

Prep Time: 16 minutes.
Cooking Time: 19 minutes.
Total Time: 35 minutes
Servings: 4
Difficulty: Show off

INGREDIENTS

- 2 cloves garlic
- 4 scallions
- ½ c baby kale
- 2 15-oz cans of chickpeas, drained and rinsed
- 1 tsp grated lemon zest
- 2 tbsp all-purpose flour
- 1 tsp ground cumin
- 1 tsp ground coriander
- ½ tsp salt

DIRECTIONS

1. In a food processor, pulse the garlic, scallion whites, and ½ cup of baby kale until everything is finely chopped. Add the chickpeas, lemon zest, flour, cumin, coriander, and ½ tsp salt. Pulse the falafel ingredients until well combined. Form the mixture into 24 2-tbsp balls.
2. Heat the air fryer to 160 °C/320 °F and brush the inside of the air fryer basket with oil. Add 12 of the falafel balls, ensuring that they do not touch, and air fry for 15 minutes.
3. Brush the falafel with 1 tbsp oil, then turn up the air fryer temperature setting to 200 °C/400 °F and air fryer until a deep golden colour, about 4 minutes.
4. Repeat with the remaining falafel.
5. Serve over a heap of salad greens or wrapped in a pita.

Nutrition Information

Calories 347, Fat 16 g, Saturates 2.5, Sodium 805 mg, Protein 14 g, Carbs 40 g, Fibre 12 g

Spice-Roasted Cauliflower with Green Beans (Vegan)

Prep Time: 12 minutes
Cooking Time: 13 minutes
Total Time: 25 minutes
Servings: 4
Difficulty: Show off

INGREDIENTS

- 1 c long-grain white rice
- 2 tbsp olive oil
- 1 tbsp red wine vinegar
- 1 tbsp tomato paste
- 2 tsp garam masala
- 1 tsp brown sugar
- ⅛ tsp cayenne
- Kosher salt
- 1 medium head cauliflower, cut into florets
- 6 cloves garlic, crushed
- 1 onion, cut into thick wedges
- 0.25 kg green beans, trimmed and halved
- Cilantro, chopped for serving

DIRECTIONS

1. Heat the air fryer to 185 °C/370 °F.
2. Add the cauliflower florets to a bowl with the brown sugar, oil, and the spices. Toss the cauliflower to coat it evenly. Add in the garlic and onion, and toss again.
3. Transfer the veggies to the air fryer basket and air fry until they are roasted well, about 8 minutes.
4. Add the green beans to the basket, and toss everything together to combine. Air fry all of the vegetables are tender, about 5 additional minutes.
5. Transfer the vegetables to a platter and serve with rice and a sprinkle of cilantro.

Nutrition Information

Calories 314, Fat 8 g, Saturates 1 g, Sugar 1 g, Sodium 388 mg, Protein 7 g, Carbs 55 g, Fibre 5 g

Air Fryer Tostones with Cilantro Dip (Vegan)

Prep Time: 17 minutes
Cooking Time: 8 minutes
Additional Time: 20 minutes
Total Time: 45 minutes
Servings: 4
Difficulty: Not too tricky

INGREDIENTS

Tostones
- 3 green plantains
- 2 tbsp lime juice
- Kosher salt
- 3 tbsp canola oil
- ¼ tsp smoked paprika

Cilantro Dip
- 1 ½ c cilantro
- ½ ripe hass avocado
- ½ serrano chile, chopped
- 1 clove garlic
- 1 scallion (green part) roughly chopped
- 2 tbsp lime juice
- 1 tbsp white vinegar
- ¼ tsp agave
- Kosher salt

DIRECTIONS

1. Peel the plantains by cutting 2 slits down the sides, just deep enough to cut through the peel. Peel the peel back in sections. Cut the plantain into coins, 1 cm thick.
2. In a large bowl, stir the lime juice, 2 tsp and 4 cups of water until the salt dissolves. Add in the plantains and let them soak for 20 minutes.
3. While the plantains are soaking, make the dip. In a blender, puree the cilantro, avocado, serrano chile, garlic, scallion, lime juice, vinegar, and agave. Add ¼-½ cup water, if needed, until the dip is smooth. Season the dip with salt until it matches your taste.
4. Heat the air fryer to 170 °C/340 °F, drain the plantains, and toss them in a bowl with 1 tbsp olive oil.
5. Transfer the plantains to the air fryer basket in a single layer, ensuring that they don't touch. Cook them for 9 minutes, flipping halfway through.
6. Transfer the tostones to a work surface that is lined with parchment paper. Using a heavy glass, firmly smash each one until about ½ cm thick.
7. Heat the air fryer to 200 °C/400 °F, brush each side of the tostones with oil, and sprinkle them with salt.
8. Transfer the plantains to the air fryer, separating them from each other. Cook them until the edges of the plantains start to brown, about 3-4 minutes. Flip the plantains, then cook for 4 more minutes until golden brown.

Nutrition Information

Calories 350, Fat 19 g, Saturates 6 g,
Sugar 1 g, Sodium 391 mg, Protein 42 g,
Carbs 1 g, Fibre 1 g

Peanut Sauce Soba with Crispy Tofu (Vegan)

Prep Time: 27 minutes
Cooking Time: 18 minutes
Additional Time: 45 minutes
Total Time: 1 hour 20 minutes
Servings: 4
Difficulty: Show off

INGREDIENTS

- 2 340 g packages of extra-firm tofu, drained
- 3 tbsp canola oil
- 2 tsp grated garlic
- 2 ½ tbsp low-sodium soy sauce
- 3 tbsp natural, smooth peanut butter
- 1 tbsp agave
- 1 tbsp fresh lime juice
- ¼ c hot water
- ¼ tsp grated ginger
- 1 tsp sriracha
- 1 tbsp toasted sesame oil
- 2/3 c cornstarch
- 225 g soba noodles, cooked according to package directions
- 142 g baby spinach

DIRECTIONS

1. Pat the tofu dry with paper towels, then cut them into 2 cm cubes.
2. In a small bowl, whisk the canola oil, half of the garlic, and 1 tbsp soy sauce. Transfer 1/3 of the mixture into a baking dish, coating the bottom evenly. Add the tofu, then pour the remaining marinade on top. Turn the tofu to coat, and let it sit for 45 minutes.
3. Combine the peanut butter, agave, and lime juice in a medium bowl with the remaining soy sauce. Whisk in the hot water gradually to emulsify. Whisk in the ginger, sriracha, sesame oil, and garlic, then set aside.
4. Heat the air fryer to 200 °C/400 °F.
5. Dredge the tofu through cornstarch. Coat it evenly, then shake off the excess. Add the tofu cubes to the air fryer basket, making sure that each piece is spaced apart. Air fry for 15-18 minutes, shaking the basket twice during the cooking time.
6. In a large bowl, toss the warm soba noodles with baby spinach and peanut sauce. Top with crispy tofu.

Nutrition Information

Calories 697, Fat 30 g, Saturates 4 g, Sodium 562 mg, Protein 33 g, Carbs 79 g, Fibre 4 g

Scallion Pancake

Prep Time: 12 minutes
Cooking Time: 8 minutes
Total Time: 20 minutes
Servings: 8
Difficulty: Not too tricky

INGREDIENTS

- ¼ cup low-sodium soy sauce
- 2 tbsp rice vinegar
- 2 tsp sambal style chilli paste
- 1 tsp sugar
- 1 4-cm piece fresh ginger, peeled and cut into matchsticks
- 1 400 g package round dumpling wrappers
- ¼ c sesame oil
- 8 scallions, chopped
- 8 tbsp canola oil

DIRECTIONS

1. Slice the flank steak into thin strips, cutting against In a small bowl, whisk together the soy sauce, rice vinegar, chilli paste, and sugar. Stir in the ginger and set aside.
2. On a cutting board, place 1 dumpling wrapper, brush the top of it with sesame oil, and scatter 2 tsp scallions on top. Top it with the second dumpling wrapper, and press on it to adhere. Repeat with the sesame oil, scallions, and wrappers until you have made a stack of 6 wrappers. Repeat this 6-wrapper-stack process 8 times.
3. Brush both sides of the stacks with canola oil, then place 4 stacks in the air fryer at a time.
4. Heat the air fryer to 200 °C/400 °F and air fry the scallion pancakes for 3-4 minutes. Flip the pancakes over with tongs, then cook for an additional 3-4 minutes. Repeat with the remaining stacks.

Nutrition Information

Calories 254, Fat 13 g, Saturates 7 g, Sugar 2 g, Sodium 359 mg, Protein 5 g, Carbs 39 g, Fibre 2 g

Blistered Snap Peas

Prep Time: 9 minutes
Cooking Time: 6 minutes
Total Time: 15 minutes
Servings: 4
Difficulty: Not too tricky

INGREDIENTS

- 0.5 kg snap peas, strings removed
- 2 tbsp olive oil
- ½ tsp gochugaru
- Kosher salt
- ½ lemon, plus wedges for serving
- Cilantro, optional

DIRECTIONS

1. Heat the air fryer to 200 °C/400 °F.
2. In a large bowl, toss the snap peas with oil, gochujang, and ½ tsp salt.
3. Toss the snap peas into the air fryer basket and air fry until slightly-charred, about 5-6 minutes. Squeeze some lemon juice on top.

Nutrition Information

Calories 111, Fat 7 g, Saturates 1 g,
Sodium 245 mg, Protein 4 g, Carbs 10 g,
Fibre 3 g

Poblano and Black Bean Loaded Baked Potato

Prep Time: 10 minutes
Cooking Time: 47 minutes
Total Time: 57 minutes
Servings: 4
Difficulty: Not too tricky

INGREDIENTS

- 4 medium russet potatoes, scrubbed and dried
- Olive oil
- Kosher salt
- 2 poblano peppers, cut into small pieces
- 1 can of black beans
- ½ tsp ground cumin
- ¼ tsp smoked paprika
- 1/3 c sour cream
- 1/2 tsp lime zest
- 2 tsp lime juice
- 1 large plum tomato, seeded and chopped

DIRECTIONS

1. Air fry potatoes at 200 °C/400 °F until tender, 35-40 minutes. Flip the potatoes once, about halfway through.
2. Meanwhile, toss the poblanos with 1 tsp oil and ¼ tsp salt. In another bowl, mix the beans with cumin, paprika, ¼ tsp salt, and ½ tsp oil.
3. Remove the cooked potatoes from the air fryer and transfer them to a plate.
4. Add the poblanos to the air fryer and cook until tender, about 5 minutes. Transfer them to the bowl with the beans and fold to combine. Split the potatoes, add shredded cheese (optional), and the bean-poblano mixture.
5. Return the loaded potatoes to the air fryer and air fry until the cheese has just melted and the beans have warmed through about 2 minutes.
6. Top with sour cream, tomato, and lime zest.

Nutrition Information

Calories 428, Fat 11 g, Saturates 3 g,
Sodium 42 mg, Protein 15 g, Carbs 71 g,
Fibre 13 g

Buffalo Cauliflower Bites

Prep Time: 15 minutes
Cooking Time: 30 minutes
Total Time: 45 minutes
Servings: 4
Difficulty: Show off

INGREDIENTS

Dip
- ¾ c sour cream
- 2 tsp lemon juice
- ¼ tsp kosher salt
- ¼ tsp pepper
- ½ tsp buffalo wing sauce
- 1 large scallion, finely chopped
- 1/3 c blue cheese, crumbled

Buffalo Sauce
- 1/3 cup buffalo wing sauce
- 1 tbsp canola oil
- ½ tsp agave

Cauliflower
- ½ c rice flour
- ¼ corn starch
- ¼ tsp baking powder
- ¼ tsp kosher salt
- ½ c + 2 tbsp cold seltzer
- 1 kg head cauliflower, trimmed and cut into 3 cm florets
- Canola oil for brushing

DIRECTIONS

1. Make the dip: in a bowl, combine all of the ingredients and refrigerate until ready.
2. Make the buffalo sauce: Whisk all ingredients together in a bowl, then set aside.
3. Make the cauliflower: heat the air fryer to 200 °C/400 °F. In a separate bowl, whisk together the rice flour, cornstarch, baking powder, and salt. Add in the seltzer and cauliflower, tossing to coat.
4. Brush the air fryer basket with canola oil. Working in 2 batches, add the cauliflower to the basket and cook for 10 minutes. After 10 minutes, shake the basket, then cook for an additional 5 minutes. The cauliflower should be nice and crispy.
5. Toss the cauliflower in the buffalo sauce, then serve with the dip immediately.

Nutrition Information

Calories 286, Fat 16 g, Saturates 6 g
Sodium 1075 mg, Protein 6 g, Carbs 31 g,
Fibre 3 g

Air Fryer Butternut Squash Soup

Prep Time: 15 minutes
Cooking Time: 30 minutes
Total Time: 45 minutes
Servings: 6
Difficulty: Not too tricky

INGREDIENTS

- 1 kg butternut squash, peeled and cut into 2 cm chunks
- 2 medium carrots cut into 2 cm pieces
- 1 large onion, cut into thick wedges
- 4 garlic cloves, 2 whole and 2 thinly sliced
- 1 Fresno Chile, seeded
- 4 sprigs of fresh thyme
- 4 tbsp olive oil, divided
- Salt, to taste
- 2 tbsp pepitas
- ¼ tsp smoked paprika

DIRECTIONS

1. In a large bowl, toss the squash, carrots, onion, whale garlic cloves, chile, and thyme in 2 tbsp olive oil and ¾ tsp salt.
2. Transfer to the air fryer basket at 200 °C/400 °F, shaking the basket on occasion until the vegetables are tender, which should be about 30 minutes.
3. Discard the thyme.
4. While the air fryer is cooking, cook the sliced garlic and 2 tbsp oil in a small skillet on medium heat until the garlic starts to brown around the edges. Add the pepitas and paprika and a pinch of salt. Transfer it to another bowl.
5. Transfer all but ½ cup of squash to the blender with 1 cup of water. Puree the vegetables, gradually adding 3 more cups of water. Puree until the soup is smooth.

Nutrition Information

Calories 280, Fat 16 g, Saturates 3 g,
Sodium 425 mg, Protein 5 g, Carbs 36 g,
Fibre 7 g

Air Fryer Roasted Cauliflower Soup (Vegetarian)

Prep Time: 5 minutes
Cooking Time: 30 minutes
Total Time: 35 minutes
Servings: 4
Difficulty: Not too tricky

INGREDIENTS

- 1 tbsp olive oil
- 400 g cauliflower, chopped, leaves and stalk included
- 4 spring onions, roughly chopped
- 1 stalk celery, chopped
- 2 sprigs of fresh thyme
- Large handful kale
- 100 g stale crusty bread, cut into cubes
- 1 vegetable stock cube
- 100 mL single cream

DIRECTIONS

1. Preheat the air fryer to a 200 °C/400 °F temperature.
2. Add the cauliflower, spring onion, celery, and thyme to a bowl with olive oil. Season the cauliflower with salt and pepper, then toss to combine.
3. Add the above vegetables to the air fryer basket and cook them for 20-25 minutes until they are softened and brown. D the kale, then cook for an additional 1 minute.
4. Remove the vegetables from the basket, and discard the thyme. Place the vegetables in the blender and let sit for 5 minutes to cool.
5. Place the crusty bread cubes in the air fryer basket, and cook for 3-5 minutes until crunchy and slightly browned.
6. Boil a kettle and make the stock cube with 800 mL water. Pour ½ the stock into the blender, then run it with the vegetables in the blender until smooth. Add the rest of the broth and cream into the blender and incorporate.
7. Divide the soup between the soup bowls, top with croutons and a little bit of cream.

Nutrition Information

Calories 193, Fat 10 g, Saturates 4 g,
Sugar 5 g, Sodium 1 g, Protein 6 g,
Carbs 19 g, Fibre 3 g

Air Fryer Crispy Tofu (Vegan)

Prep Time: 5 minutes
Cooking Time: 17 minutes
Total Time: 22 minutes
Servings: 2
Difficulty: Easy

INGREDIENTS

- 280 g extra firm tofu, drained and cut into 1-2 cm cubes
- 1 tbsp cornflour
- ¼ tsp white pepper
- Pinch chilli flakes
- 1 tsp sesame seeds
- 1 tsp vegetable oil
- 1 tbsp agave
- 1 tsp rice wine vinegar
- 1 clove garlic, crushed

DIRECTIONS

1. Preheat the air fryer temperature setting to 200 °C/400 °F.
2. Pat the drained tofu dry and add it to a bowl. Sprinkle the cornflour, white pepper, chilli flakes, and sesame seeds over it, in addition to a dash of salt and pepper. Toss the seasonings and tofu together until well-coated. Drizzle with oil and toss to coat.
3. Add the tofu to the air fryer, spacing them out. Cook the tofu for 15 minutes, shaking the basket every 5 minutes or so. You want the tofu to be golden and crisp.
4. Add the sauce ingredients to a separate, heat-safe bowl and microwave for 1-2 minutes, stirring regularly. Serve alongside the crispy tofu.

Nutrition Information

Calories 292, Fat 13 g, Saturates 2 g, Sugar 10 g, Sodium 2 g, Protein 24 g, Carbs 17 g, Fibre 3 g

Air Fryer Kale Chips

Prep Time: 2 minutes
Cooking Time: 8 minutes
Total Time: 10 minutes
Servings: 1
Difficulty: Easy

INGREDIENTS

- 50 g kale, washed, dried and shredded
- ½ tbsp olive oil
- ½ tsp sea salt

DIRECTIONS

1. Spray or drizzle the olive oil on the kale and use your hands to evenly coat all of the leaves.
2. Sprinkle the kale with ½ of the sea salt.
3. Transfer the kale leaves to the air fryer basket and add a metal rack on top to prevent the leaves from flying about.
4. Cook the kale for 5-8 minutes in the air fryer at 190 °C/380 °F. Check on the kale frequently to make sure they are not burning. The kale should be perfectly crispy before the 8-minute mark.

Nutrition Information

Calories 74, Fat 7 g, Saturates 1 g, Sugar 1 g, Sodium 1174 mg, Protein 1 g, Carbs 3 g, Fibre 1 g

Air Fryer Chickpeas

Prep Time: 2 minutes
Cooking Time: 15 minutes
Total Time: 17 minutes
Servings: 1
Difficulty: Easy

INGREDIENTS

- 1 400 g can chickpeas, drained and rinsed
- 1 tbsp olive oil
- 2 tsp seasoning of choice (peri, smoked paprika, garlic and herb, curry powder, etc.)

DIRECTIONS

1. Toss the chickpeas with olive oil and herb spice of your choice.
2. Transfer the seasoned chickpeas to the air fryer basket and cook for 15 minutes at 200 °C/400 °F, shaking the basket 2 or 3 times during the cooking time.
3. The chickpeas should be hard and crispy when they are ready.

Nutrition Information

Calories 389, Fat 12 g, Saturates 1 g, Sugar 10 g, Sodium 1033 mg, Protein 18 g, Carbs 55 g, Fibre 15 g

Air Fryer Tahini Black Bean Fritters

Prep Time: 10 minutes
Cooking Time: 15 minutes
Total Time: 25 minutes
Servings: 4
Difficulty: Show off

INGREDIENTS

- 1 425 g can black beans, rinsed and drained
- 113 oz baby bella mushrooms, trimmed
- ½ small yellow onion
- ½ c breadcrumbs
- 2 tbsp white miso
- ½ tsp garlic powder
- ½ tsp smoked paprika
- 3 tbsp tahini
- ½ tsp kosher salt
- Olive oil cooking spray
- 2 tbsp dill, finely chopped
- 2 tbsp water
- 2 tbsp white wine vinegar
- Sliced cherry tomatoes or cucumbers for serving

DIRECTIONS

1. Mash the beans, mushrooms, onion, paprika, breadcrumbs, miso, garlic powder, 1 tbsp tahini, and ¼ tsp salt in a bowl until combined. Form the bean mixture into 8 evenly-sized patties.
2. Lightly coat the air fryer basket with spray oil. Working in batches, arrange the patties in the air fryer basket so that they are evenly spaced. Spray them with cooking spray.
3. Cook the patties at 200 °C/400 °F for 15 minutes, flipping them halfway through. You want the patties to be crispy and brown.
4. In a bowl, mix the dill, water, vinegar, and remaining 2 tbsp tahini and ¼ tsp salt together until smooth. If you want your dressing to be thinner, you can add more water.
5. Drizzle the patties with the tahini dressing and top with the chopped cucumbers and tomatoes.

Nutrition Information

Calories 175, Fat 7 g, Saturates 1 g, Sugar 1 g, Sodium 6 mg, Protein 12 g, Carbs 23 g, Fibre 1 g

This page is for your notes

CHAPTER 7

SIDE DISHES AND APPETISERS RECIPES

Air Fryer Potato Wedges

Prep Time: 5 minutes
Cooking Time: 20 minutes
Total Time: 25 minutes
Servings: 4
Difficulty: Easy

INGREDIENTS

- 4 large potatoes, cut into wedges
- 1-2 tbsp oil
- 1 tsp seasoning

DIRECTIONS

1. Wash and scrub each potato before cutting them into wedges.
2. Soak the potato wedges in cold water for up to 30 minutes or rinse them under cold water after they are cut. This will help remove the starches from the potatoes.
3. Pat the wedges dry with a kitchen roll or clean tea towel.
4. Brush the wedges with a thin coating of oil. This step is optional if you prefer making oil-free wedges.
5. Season the wedges according to your taste preferences. Some of our favourite seasoning options include salt, paprika, cayenne, or curry powder.
6. Place the potato wedges into the air fryer basket. Depending on the size of your air fryer, you may need to cook them in batches in order to cook all of the wedges.
7. Cook the wedges at 200 °C/400F ° for 20 minutes, removing and shaking the basket every 5 minutes in order to ensure even cooking.
8. Cook the potatoes until the wedges are crispy on the outside. If you cook many wedges at the same time, it may take longer.
9. Remove the wedges from the air fryer basket and add more seasoning if necessary.

Nutrition Information

Calories 341, Fat 7 g, Saturates 1 g,
Sugar 4 g, Sodium 410mg, Protein 8 g,
Carbs 63 g, Fibre 7 g

Air Fryer Chips

Prep Time: 10 minutes
Cooking Time: 25 minutes
Total Time: 35 minutes
Servings: 3-5
Difficulty: Easy

INGREDIENTS

- 600 g potatoes, sliced
- Oil (optional)
- Seasoning

DIRECTIONS

1. Slice the potatoes up, thick for regular chips or thin for french fries. Whether or not you want to peel the potatoes is up to you. If you do decide to leave the skin on, be sure to give them a good scrub.
2. Preheat the air fryer to a 200 °C/400 °F temperature.
3. Wash the potatoes in cold water in order to remove the layer of starch.
4. Pat the potatoes dry with a clean kitchen towel or tea towel.
5. (Optional) Spray the potatoes with some oil.
6. Sprinkle the potatoes with your choice of seasoning. Some of our favourite seasoning options are chip seasoning, curry powder, paprika, salt, garlic, and/ or pepper.
7. Transfer the seasoned potatoes to the air fryer basket.
8. Cook the chips for 20 to 25 minutes, checking on them regularly and shaking the basket periodically. Depending on the thickness of the chip and how crispy you prefer your chips to be, you may want to cook them a little longer.

Nutrition Information

Calories 171, Fat 4 g, Saturates 0 g,
Sugar 2 g, Sodium 1110 mg, Protein 4 g,
Carbs 32 g, Fibre 3 g

Air Fryer Roast Potatoes

Prep Time: 10 minutes
Cooking Time: 25 minutes
Total Time: 35 minutes
Servings: 4
Difficulty: Easy

INGREDIENTS

- 8 medium potatoes, peeled and cubed or chopped
- 1 tbsp olive oil

DIRECTIONS

1. Preheat the air fryer to 180 °C/360 °F.
2. Peel and chop up the potatoes. The smaller the potatoes are cut, the faster they will cook in the air fryer.
3. Spray or brush the potatoes with 1 tbsp of oil. Make sure that all of the potatoes are coated.
4. Put the cubed potatoes in the air fryer basket, and slide the basket into the fryer.
5. Cook the potatoes in the air fryer basket for 25 minutes. Check them periodically and give them a good shake every 5 minutes or so.

Nutrition Information

Calories 196, Fat 7 g, Saturates 1 g,
Sugar 1 g, Sodium 453 mg, Protein 4 g,
Carbs 30 g, Fibre 4 g

Air Fryer Garlic and Herb New Potatoes

Prep Time: 5 minutes
Cooking Time: 20 minutes
Total Time: 25 minutes
Servings: 4
Difficulty: Not too tricky

INGREDIENTS

- 1 kg potatoes
- 2-3 sprigs rosemary
- Handful of fresh parsley
- 2 tbsp garlic powder
- 2 tsp salt
- 2 tbsp olive oil

DIRECTIONS

1. Chop the potatoes into even-sized cubes.
2. Finely chop the parsley and rosemary leaves.
3. Place the chopped potatoes in a large bowl and sprinkle the chopped herbs, garlic powder, and salt. Drizzle the potatoes with olive oil and mix until the potatoes are well-coated.
4. Cook the chopped and seasoned potatoes in the air fryer at 200 °C/400 °F for 20 minutes. Shake the potatoes halfway through the cooking time (10 minutes). You may need to cook the herb potatoes in two batches in order for the potatoes to cook evenly.

Nutrition Information

Calories 307, Fat 7 g, Saturates 1 g, Sugar 3 g, Sodium 197 mg, Protein 7 g, Carbs 56 g, Fibre 6 g

Air Fryer Sweet Potato Fries

Prep Time: 5 minutes
Cooking Time: 12 minutes
Total Time: 17 minutes
Servings: 2
Difficulty: Easy

INGREDIENTS

- 1 large sweet potato (approximately 350 g)
- 1 tbsp grapeseed oil (or oil of choice, including olive oil, coconut oil, or avocado oil)
- 2 tsp spice/seasoning mix (some of our favourites are paprika, cayenne, garlic, and pepper)
- Salt for seasoning once cooked

DIRECTIONS

1. Preheat the air fryer temperature to 180 °C/360 °F.
2. Peel the sweet potato (optional).
3. Slice the sweet potato into thin strips.
4. Drizzle the potatoes with oil, coating as many of the fries as possible.
5. Sprinkle the spice mix over the fries and toss to coat them fully.
6. Lay the prepared fries in the air fryer basket, ensuring that they are spread apart enough to create space for even cooking and air circulation.
7. Cook the fries for 12 minutes, checking on them halfway. Shake the basket to turn them over.

Nutrition Information

Calories 149, Fat 4 g, Saturates 1 g, Sugar 5 g, Sodium 653 mg, Protein 2 g, Carbs 27 g, Fibre 4 g

Air Fryer Sweet Potato Wedges

Prep Time: 10 minutes
Cooking Time: 20 minutes
Total Time: 30 minutes
Servings: 4
Difficulty: Easy

INGREDIENTS

- 1 kg potatoes, cut into chunks
- 1 medium cabbage, shredded
- 5 tbsp butter
- 20 g chives, chopped
- 4 tbsp milk
- Salt, to taste
- Pepper, to taste
- 150 g cheddar cheese, grated

DIRECTIONS

1. Cook the potatoes and cabbage, either steamed or boiled and prepared in separate pots.
2. Preheat your air fryer to a temperature of 180 °C/360 °F.
3. Drain and mash the potatoes and mix with the milk and butter until smooth. Season the mashed potatoes with salt and pepper to your taste.
4. Drain the cabbage, and season it with salt and pepper to taste.
5. In a large mixing bowl, mix the cabbage, mashed potatoes, and chives with a wooden spoon until well incorporated.
6. Taste the vegetable mixture to see if it needs any additional seasoning.
7. Spoon the mixture into a large, ovenproof dish and smooth down the top. You may have to make two separate batches, depending on the size capacity of your air fryer.
8. Add a layer of grated cheese on top, and cook in the air fryer for 15-20 minutes or until golden brown on top.

Nutrition Information

Calories 359, Fat 19 g, Saturates 11 g, Sugar 7 g, Sodium 312 mg, Protein 12 g, Carbs 39 g, Fibre 8 g

Air Fryer Yorkshire Pudding

Prep Time: 5 minutes
Cooking Time: 15 minutes
Resting Time: 30 minutes
Total Time: 50 minutes
Servings: 12
Difficulty: Not too tricky

INGREDIENTS

- 130 g plain/all-purpose flour
- ½ tsp salt
- 3 large eggs
- 240 mL milk
- 3 tbsp vegetable cooking oil

DIRECTIONS

1. Measure the flour into a medium mixing bowl and add a pinch of salt, stirring to combine.
2. Crack the eggs into the mixing bowl and add a splash of milk. Whisk the ingredients together.
3. Gradually add the remaining milk, thoroughly mixing in-between additions. Mix until you have achieved a smooth batter, and let the batter rest for 30 minutes or overnight in the refrigerator.
4. Place a silicone muffin tin in the air fryer basket, add ½ tsp of the vegetable baking oil to each tin insert, and preheat the air fryer at a temperature of 200 °C/400 °F for 10 minutes.
5. Stir the batter well before making the puddings. Evenly pour the batter halfway into each tin, working quickly.
6. Air fry the puddings for 10 minutes or until the tops of the puddings are golden brown and puffed-up on top.
7. Use kitchen tongs to flip them over at the 10-minute mark, and flip them over for 5 more minutes of cooking.

Nutrition Information

Calories 98, Fat 5 g, Saturates 1 g, Sugar 1 g, Sodium 121 mg, Protein 3 g, Carbs 9 g, Fibre 0.3g

Air Fryer Pigs in a Blanket

Prep Time: 5 minutes
Cooking Time: 12 minutes
Total Time: 17 minutes
Servings: 4
Difficulty: Not too tricky

INGREDIENTS

- 8 rashers of streaky bacon, smoked or unsmoked
- 8 pork chipolatas

DIRECTIONS

1. Wrap one slice of bacon around each chipolata and arrange them in a single layer in the air fryer basket.
2. Cook the pigs in a blanket at 180 °C/360 °F for 10-12 minutes until the bacon and chipolata are cooked through. Cook the pigs in a blanket for a couple of extra minutes if you prefer your bacon to be extra-crispy.

Nutrition Information

Calories 314, Fat 24 g, Saturates 9 g,
Sugar 1 g, Sodium 3 g, Protein 18 g,
Carbs 6 g, Fibre 1 g

Air Fryer Brussel Sprouts

Prep Time: 5 minutes
Cooking Time: 15 minutes
Total Time: 20 minutes
Servings: 4-6
Difficulty: Easy

INGREDIENTS

- 350 g fresh Brussel sprouts, or 250 g if frozen
- 1 tsp vegetable oil
- Chopped cooked bacon, chopped roasted hazelnuts, or chilli flakes, to serve

DIRECTIONS

1. Preheat the air fryer to a temperature of 180 °C/360 °F.
2. If you are using fresh brussel sprouts, trim them. Drizzle the sprouts with the vegetable oil and season as desired. Toss them well in order to coat the sprouts evenly.
3. Arrange the sprouts in the air fryer basket in a single, even layer. This is to ensure that they are cooked evenly. Cook the sprouts for 10-15 minutes, mixing them about halfway through the cooking time.
4. If you are cooking the brussel sprouts from frozen, place the sprouts in the air fryer basket in an even layer, and cook them for 10-15 minutes, depending on how coloured you like them to be.

Nutrition Information

Calories 36, Fat 1 g, Saturates 0 g,
Sugar 2 g, Sodium 0g, Protein 2 g,
Carbs 2 g, Fibre 3 g

Air Fryer Roasted Peppers

Prep Time: 5 minutes
Cooking Time: 12 minutes
Total Time: 17 minutes
Servings: 4
Difficulty: Easy

INGREDIENTS

- 3 sweet bell peppers, chopped into bite-sized pieces
- 1 tbsp olive oil
- ½ tsp sea salt

DIRECTIONS

1. Spray or drizzle the peppers with olive oil and sea salt or any other seasonings of your choice.
2. Transfer the peppers to the air fryer basket.
3. Set the air fryer temperature to 200 °C/400 °F and cook the peppers for 10-12 minutes. Check on the peppers frequently, shaking the basket each time. The peppers should be soft and slightly browned.

Nutrition Information

Calories 54, Fat 4 g, Saturates 1 g, Sugar 2 g, Sodium 266 mg, Protein 1 g, Carbs 6 g, Fibre 1 g

Air Fryer Baked Potatoes

Prep Time: 2 minutes
Cooking Time: 50 minutes
Total Time: 52 minutes
Servings: 4
Difficulty: Easy

INGREDIENTS

- 4 baking potatoes, about 250 g each
- ½ tbsp sunflower oil
- Toppings of your choice: butter, cheese, baked beans, tuna, etc.

DIRECTIONS

1. Wash and scrub your potatoes, and then pat dry with a paper towel.
2. Transfer the potatoes to a plate, and drizzle with oil. Rub the oil into the skin of the potatoes with your hands, coating the potatoes well. Season the potatoes with salt and pepper; the salt will help the skin crisp up.
3. Arrange the whole potatoes in a single layer in the air fryer basket, and ensure that they are not overcrowding each other. Set the temperature to 200 °C/400 °F and cook the potatoes for 40-50 minutes, or until a sharp knife can puncture the potatoes with ease. Check the potatoes at the 20-minute mark and flip the potatoes over for even browning.
4. When the potatoes are done, the skin should be crisp, and the inside should be light and fluffy.

Nutrition Information

Calories 206, Fat 2 g, Saturates 0 g, Sugar 3 g, Sodium 0 g, Protein 5 g, Carbs 40 g, Fibre 5 g

Air Fryer Halloumi

Prep Time: 2 minutes
Cooking Time: 15 minutes
Total Time: 17 minutes
Servings: 6
Difficulty: Not too tricky

INGREDIENTS

- 225 g halloumi, cut into 1 cm x 6 cm thick slices
- 1 tsp olive oil
- 1 tsp seasoning of choice (we suggest smoked paprika or mixed herbs)

DIRECTIONS

1. Heat the air fryer to a temperature of 200 °C/400 °F.
2. Carefully pat the halloumi dry using a clean kitchen cloth or paper towel. Brush the cheese with oil, and season with salt, pepper, and/or any of your favourite seasonings.
3. Add the halloumi to the air fryer basket and cook for 8 minutes or until it begins to brown. Flip the halloumi over and cook for an additional 2-5 minutes until it is a nice golden colour.

Nutrition Information

Calories 121, Fat 9 g, Saturates 6 g,
Sugar 1 g, Sodium 1 g, Protein 9 g,
Carbs 1 g, Fibre 0 g

Air Fryer Garlic Mushrooms

Prep Time: 5 minutes
Cooking Time: 9 minutes
Total Time: 14 minutes
Servings: 2
Difficulty: Easy

INGREDIENTS

- 250 g button mushrooms
- 1 garlic bulb
- Fresh rosemary
- Extra virgin olive oil spray
- ½ tsp garlic powder
- Salt, to taste
- Pepper, to taste
- 1 tbsp butter

DIRECTIONS

1. Slice your mushrooms lengthwise into thirds.
2. Peel the garlic bulb into many garlic cloves.
3. Load the garlic and mushrooms into the air fryer basket with the rosemary. Spray the vegetables with extra virgin olive oil; then air fry for 6 minutes at 180 °C/360 °F.
4. Spray the mushrooms again with extra virgin olive oil and cook at 200 °C/400 °F for an additional 3 minutes.
5. Melt some butter in the microwave, then toss the mushrooms in the butter just before serving.

Nutrition Information

Calories 82, Fat 6 g, Saturates 4 g,
Sugar 3 g, Sodium 57 mg, Protein 4 g,
Carbs 5 g, Fibre 1 g

Air Fryer Slimming World Chips and Gravy

Prep Time: 0 minutes
Cooking Time: 15 minutes
Total Time: 15 minutes
Servings: 2
Difficulty: Easy

INGREDIENTS

- 250 g bag frozen Slimming World chips
- Slimming World onion gravy
- salt, to taste
- Vinegar, to taste

DIRECTIONS

1. Load the frozen slimming world chips into the air fryer, and cook for 5 minutes at 160 °C/320 °F. While the chips are cooking, pour the gravy into a ramekin.
2. Remove the chips from the air fryer after the timer has gone off, and toss the chips in a bowl with salt and vinegar.
3. Add the gravy-filled ramekin into the air fryer, and pour the chips back into the basket around the ramekin. Cook the chips and gravy for an additional 5 minutes at the same temperature.
4. Stir the gravy and shake the chips in the basket, then cook for a final 5 minutes at 200 °C/400 °F in order to make the chips crispy.

Nutrition Information

Calories 325, Fat 19 g, Saturates 6 g, Sugar 0 g, Sodium 613 mg, Protein 4 g, Carbs 38 g, Fibre 6 g

Corn on the Cob

Prep Time: 3 minutes
Cooking Time: 15 minutes
Total Time: 18 minutes
Servings: 2
Difficulty: Easy

INGREDIENTS

- 2 corn on the cob
- 2 tsp water
- Spray oil

DIRECTIONS

1. Place the corn on the cob onto a sheet of foil, and pull the edges of the foil up above the corn to make a little boat. Add 1 tsp of water to each foil packet.
2. Wrap the foil closed around the corn.
3. Place the foil-covered corn in the air fryer basket at 190 °C/380 °F and cook for 10 minutes.
4. Remove the foil, spray the corn with oil, and place the corn back in the air fryer without the foil for an additional 5 minutes.

Nutrition Information

Calories 77, Fat 1 g, Saturates 0 g, Sugar 6 g, Sodium 14 mg, Protein 3 g, Carbs 17 g, Fibre 2 g

Air Fryer Parsnips

Prep Time: 5 minutes
Cooking Time: 12 minutes
Total Time: 17 minutes
Servings: 4
Difficulty: Not too tricky

INGREDIENTS

- 4 parsnips
- 1 tbsp oil
- Salt, to taste
- Black pepper, to taste

DIRECTIONS

1. Wash and peel the parsnips and cut them down into evenly sized-batons.
2. Add the parsnip batons to a large bowl and drizzle them with olive oil. Season the parsnips with salt and pepper or any other flavourings like honey, garlic powder, dried herbs, etc. Mix the parsnips, oil, and seasonings by hand, coating them evenly.
3. Place the parsnips in the air fryer basket in an evenly spaced layer, and cook them at 200 °C/400 °F for 6 minutes. Flip them over for even cooking, then cook for an additional 6-8 minutes.

Nutrition Information

Calories 165, Fat 4 g, Saturates 2 g,
Sugar 12 g, Sodium 16 mg, Protein 2 g,
Carbs 32 g, Fibre 8 g

Spicy Curried Potato Wedges

Prep Time: 10 minutes
Cooking Time: 35 minutes
Total Time: 45 minutes
Servings: 4
Difficulty: Not too tricky

INGREDIENTS

- 3 medium-large potatoes, about 470 g
- 1 tsp curry powder
- 2 garlic cloves, crushed
- ½ tsp salt
- ½ tsp pepper
- 2 tbsp olive oil

DIRECTIONS

1. Wash the potatoes, then cut them into wedges.
2. Place the curry powder, garlic, salt, pepper, and olive oil in a large bowl or ziplock bag. Mix the seasonings until well incorporated, then add the potato wedges, mixing to coat.
3. Place the potato wedges in the air fryer basket, allowing room for each of the wedges to cook evenly. You may have to cook multiple batches.
4. Cook the potato wedges for 15-20 minutes, turning the wedges over halfway through.

Nutrition Information

Calories 122, Fat 7 g, Saturates 1 g,
Sugar 1 g, Sodium 1 mg, Protein 2 g,
Carbs 13 g, Fibre 1 g

Air Fryer Swiss Chard

Prep Time: 0 minutes
Cooking Time: 10 minutes
Total Time: 10 minutes
Servings: 4
Difficulty: Not too tricky

INGREDIENTS

- 1 medium red onion, sliced
- 1 ½ tbsp oil
- 1 large bunch of red swiss chard, stems discarded and leaves chopped
- 2 cloves garlic, sliced

DIRECTIONS

1. Heat the air fryer to 170 °C/340 °F and toss the onion with ½ tbsp oil and a pinch of salt and pepper. Air fry for 5 minutes.
2. Toss the onion with Swiss chard, garlic, 1 tbsp oil, and ¼ tsp salt and pepper each. Air fry the mixture until the Swiss chard and onion are tender, about 5 minutes.

Nutrition Information

Calories 83, Fat 7 g, Saturates 1 g,
Sugar 1 g, Sodium 242 mg, Protein 2 g,
Carbs 4 g, Fibre 2 g

Air Fryer Jalapeno Poppers

Prep Time: 13 minutes
Cooking Time: 7 minutes
Total Time: 20 minutes
Servings: 4-6
Difficulty: Not too tricky

INGREDIENTS

- 114 g cream cheese, room temperature
- ½ cup extra sharp cheddar cheese, shredded
- 1 scallion, finely chopped
- 6 medium-large jalapenos
- Nonstick cooking spray

DIRECTIONS

1. In a medium bowl, mix together the cream cheese, cheddar, scallion, and a dash of hot sauce (optional) until smooth. Transfer the filling mixture into a plastic bag.
2. Half the jalapenos lengthwise, scraping the seeds out with a spoon.
3. Heat the air fryer to 190 °C/380 °F.
4. Snip one of the corners of the plastic bag and pipe the filling into the jalapeno halves.
5. Lightly coat the air fryer basket with cooking spray, and arrange the poppers in a single layer. Cook the poppers until the tops are browned, about 6-7 minutes.

Nutrition Information

Calories 135, Fat 12 g, Saturates 7 g,
Sodium 143 mg, Protein 4 g, Carbs 3 g,
Fibre 1 g

Roasted Asparagus with Creamy Feta

Prep Time: 5
Cooking Time: 10
Total Time: 15 minutes
Servings: 6
Difficulty: Not too tricky

INGREDIENTS

- 1 kg asparagus, trimmed
- 2 tbsp olive oil
- Kosher salt
- 227 g feta
- ½ c plain whole milk yoghourt
- 1 lemon

DIRECTIONS

1. Heat the air fryer to a temperature of 200 °C/400 °F.
2. In a large bowl, toss 0.5 kg of the asparagus with 1 tbsp olive oil and ¼ tsp of salt and pepper each.
3. Add the asparagus to the air fryer and cook for 10 minutes, shaking halfway through. Repeat for the other half of the asparagus.
4. In the food processor, blend together half of the feta and ¼ c of the yoghurt until creamy. Spread half of the mixture onto a platter.
5. Grate ½ of a lemon over the cooked asparagus in the air fryer, then use tongs to place the asparagus over the feta mixture. Serve with the remaining creamy feta on the side.

Nutrition Information

Calories 170, Fat 14 g, Saturates 7 g,
Sodium 525 mg, Protein 8 g, Carbs 6 g,
Fibre 2 g

This page is for your notes

This page is for your notes

CHAPTER 8

DESSERT RECIPES

Easy Air Fryer Scones

Prep Time: 10 minutes
Cooking Time: 8 minutes
Total Time: 18 minutes
Servings: 5
Difficulty: Easy

INGREDIENTS

- 175 g self-raising flour
- ½ tsp baking powder
- 45 g butter
- 2 tbsp caster sugar
- 85 mL milk
- A squeeze of lemon juice
- ½ tsp vanilla extract

DIRECTIONS

1. Preheat the air fryer to 200 °C/400 °F.
2. Measure out the flour, baking powder, and cubed butter into a large mixing bowl, and mix with your hands until you get a breadcrumb-like consistency.
3. Mix in the caster sugar until combined.
4. Heat the milk in the microwave for 30 seconds, then add a generous squeeze of lemon juice and measured vanilla extract. Leave the milk mixture to rest for a couple of minutes, then mix the soured milk into the flour using a cutlery knife.
5. Knead the dough in the bowl together with your hands. The dough will be sticky and soft.
6. Lightly flour your work surface, then tip over and knead the scone dough for a few seconds in order to cover it in flour. Shape the dough into a 3 cm thick disc and stamp out 5 scones with your cookie cutter. Repeat this shaping and kneading process until all of the dough is used up.
7. Brush the tops of the scones with a bit of milk, and air fry for 7-8 minutes until the scones are well-risen and golden brown.
8. Remove the scones from the fryer basket and set them out on a wire rack to cool for 10 minutes or so before serving them.

Nutrition Information

Calories 209, Fat 5 g, Saturates 1 g,
Sugar 6 g, Sodium 50 mg, Protein 7 g,
Carbs 34g, Fibre 1 g

Spotted Dick

Prep Time: 10 minutes
Cooking Time: 1 hour 30 minutes
Total Time: 1 hour 40 minutes
Servings: 6
Difficulty: Show off

INGREDIENTS

- 225 g self-raising flour
- 60 g caster sugar
- 115 g suet (or butter)
- 140 g raisins or currants
- 150 mL milk
- Grated rind of one lemon

DIRECTIONS

1. In a large mixing bowl, combine the flour, sugar, suet (or butter), dried fruit, and lemon zest.
2. Add in the milk, and stir together until a soft dough forms.
3. Transfer the mixture to a greased pudding mould or bowl and level off the top so that it is flat.
4. Cover the bowl with grease-proof paper, then a layer of aluminium foil on top.
5. Fill the bottom tray of the air fryer with water, then preheat the air fryer to 200 °C/400 °F.
6. Place the pudding mould in the air fryer basket, and cook for 25-30 minutes. Check periodically to make sure that the water in the bottom tray does not completely evaporate. The sponge is done when it gently springs back when you press on it.
7. Serve with ice cream or warm custard.

Nutrition Information

Calories 507, Fat 21 g, Saturates 12 g, Sugar 40 g, Sodium 482 mg, Protein 7 g, Carbs 77 g, Fibre 4 g

Air Fryer Victoria Sponge Cake

Prep Time: 20 minutes
Cooking Time: 35 minutes
Total Time: 55 minutes
Servings: 8
Difficulty: Not too tricky

INGREDIENTS

Cake
- 225 g self-raising flour
- 250 g granulated sugar
- 230 g unsalted butter
- 5 large eggs
- 50 g cocoa powder
- 2 tbsp extra virgin olive oil
- 8 tbsp skim milk
- 2 tbsp vanilla extract

Filling
- 180 mL heavy cream
- 2 tbsp strawberry jam

DIRECTIONS

1. Add the butter and sugar into a mixing bowl and beat until it makes a fluffy batter that is pale in colour.
2. Crack the eggs into the mixing bowl, and add the vanilla extract and olive oil to the batter. Mix this batter until smooth, then add in the milk, followed by small increments of flour. Scrape the edges of the bowl as you go, ensuring that the cake batter is smooth and without lumps.
3. Split the batter between 2 cake pans, silicone pans preferably. Air fry each cake for 10 minutes at 160 °C/320 °F, cover the cake with foil, then bake for the final 25 minutes at 150 °C/300 °F.
4. Remove the cakes from the cake moulds, then leave them to cool on a cooling rack.
5. On the bottom cake, spread the strawberry jam thinly across the face of the cake. Whip the heavy cream until you have a whipping cream. Using a piping bag, pipe the whipped cream over the jam.
6. Sandwich the second cake on top of the whipped cream, dust with icing sugar, and you are ready to eat.

Nutrition Information

Calories 61, Fat 39 g, Saturates 22 g, Sugar 36 g, Sodium 59 mg, Protein 9 g, Carbs 61 g, Fibre 3 g

Air Fryer Dark Red Velvet Cookies

Prep Time: 30 minutes
Cooking Time: 15 minutes
Total Time: 45 minutes
Servings: 30
Difficulty: Show off

INGREDIENTS

- 2 c all-purpose flour
- ½ c Dutch process cocoa powder
- 1 tsp baking soda
- 1 tsp kosher salt
- 1 c unsalted butter, room temperature
- ¾ c brown sugar, packed
- ½ c granulated sugar
- 1 large egg
- 1 tsp red gel paste food colouring
- 2 tsp pure vanilla extract
- 1 package of semisweet chocolate chips

DIRECTIONS

1. Line the bottom of the air fryer basket with a piece of parchment paper, leaving enough space around the edges for air circulation during cook time, and preheat the air fryer temperature to 150°C/300 °F.
2. In a large bowl, whisk the dry ingredients, including flour, cocoa powder, baking soda, and salt, together.
3. Using an electric mixer, beat the sugars and butter together until smooth, then add the egg, food colouring, and vanilla. Mix until well combined.
4. Add flour on a low speed, followed by the chocolate chips.
5. Scoop the dough in 2 tbsp increments onto the parchment. You will most likely need to work in batches. Leave the cookies approximately 5 cm apart.
6. Air fry the cookies for 14-15 minutes until the tops are set and slightly cracked.
7. Let the cookies sit for 5 minutes before moving them to a wire rack to cool completely.

Nutrition Information

Calories 142, Fat 6 g, Saturates 4 g,
Sugar 13 g, Sodium 96 mg, Protein 1 g,
Carbs 20 g, Fibre 1 g

Air Fryer Pumpkin Biscuits

Prep Time: 10 minutes
Cooking Time: 12 minutes
Total Time: 22 minutes
Servings: 4
Difficulty: Not too tricky

INGREDIENTS

- 1 c all-purpose flour
- 1 tbsp light brown sugar
- 1 tsp baking powder
- ¾ tsp pumpkin spice
- ½ tsp salt
- 4 tbsp unsalted butter, cold and cut into cubes
- ¼ c canned pumpkin puree
- 2 tbsp buttermilk

DIRECTIONS

1. In a medium bowl, whisk the flour, sugar, baking powder, pumpkin spice, and salt together. Use a fork to work the cubed butter into the flour mixture until it represents a coarse meal texture.
2. In a different bowl, whisk the pumpkin puree and buttermilk until combined. Pour the liquid ingredients into the dry flour mixture, stirring with a fork until the shaggy dough forms.
3. Turn the dough on a lightly floured surface and gently knead the dough until no dry spots remain. Cut the dough into 4 even square pieces and brush the tops with melted butter.
4. In the air fryer basket, arrange the dough in a well-spaced even layer. Cook at 175 °C/350 °F for 10-12 minutes. During the last 3 minutes of cooking, tent a piece of foil over the biscuits to prevent over-browning.

Nutrition Information

Calories 234, Fat 8 g, Saturates 5 g,
Sugar 5 g, Sodium 251 mg, Protein 2 g,
Carbs 22g, Fibre 1 g

Peanut Butter Molten Chocolate Cakes

Prep Time: 20 minutes
Cooking Time: 25 minutes
Total Time: 45 minutes
Servings: 6
Difficulty: Show off

INGREDIENTS

- ¾ c unsalted butter, cut into pieces
- 1/3 c granulated sugar
- 170 g semisweet chocolate chips
- 3 large eggs at room temperature
- 3 egg yolks at room temperature
- 1 tsp pure vanilla extract
- ¼ tsp salt
- 1/3 c all-purpose flour
- 1 tbsp unsweetened cocoa powder
- ½ tsp baking powder
- 1/3 c creamy peanut butter (not natural)
- 3 tbsp confectioner's sugar

DIRECTIONS

1. In a medium saucepan, bring 2 cm water to a simmer. Butter 6 ramekins and dust them with granulated sugar. Combine the semisweet chocolate chips and butter in a large, heatproof bowl and place the bowl over the simmering water to gently melt. Stir occasionally until smooth, then remove the bowl from the heat source.
2. Whisk together in a separate bowl the granulated sugar, eggs, yolks, vanilla, and salt until well combined.
3. In a smaller bowl, you can whisk together the flour, cocoa powder, and baking powder. Add the egg mixture to the chocolate, mixing until combined. Add the flour mixture in increments, whisking until smooth.de ½ the batter among the prepared ramekins.
4. In a separate bowl, mix the peanut butter and confectioner's sugar until combined. Scoop 1 tbsp into each of the half-filled ramekins. Cover with the remaining chocolate cake batter.
5. Heat the air fryer to 185 °C/370 °F. Working in batches, place the ramekins into the air fryer basket, cooking the cakes for about 8 minutes. The cakes should be puffed up and set. Allow the cakes to rest for about 2 minutes before serving.

Nutrition Information

Calories 592, Fat 45 g, Saturates 23 g,
Sodium 233 mg, Protein 10 g, Carbs 45 g,
Fibre 3 g

Air Fryer Apple Crumble

Prep Time: 10 minutes
Cooking Time: 30 minutes
Total Time: 40 minutes
Servings: 6
Difficulty: Not too tricky

INGREDIENTS

- 900 g peeled, cored, and roughly chopped Bramley apples
- 4 tsp ground cinnamon
- 40 g + 2 tbsp demerara sugar
- 100 g unsalted butter
- 200 g plain flour
- Single cream, optional

DIRECTIONS

1. Add 900 g apples to a 20 cm firm-base cake tin, adding 2 tbsp water, 2 tsp cinnamon, and 2 tbsp demerara sugar. Toss the apples well.
2. Air fry the apples in the tin at 180 °C/360 °F for 20 minutes, stirring halfway through the cooking time.
3. In a mixing bowl, mix the unsalted butter with plain flour until the mixture resembles breadcrumbs. Add 2 tsp ground cinnamon and 40 g demerara sugar.
4. Tip the crumble over the cooked apples, levelling it out. Air fry for an additional 10 minutes or until the crumble is a pale golden colour.

Nutrition Information

Calories 362, Fat 15 g, Saturates 9 g, Sugar 26 g, Sodium 0 g, Protein 4 g, Carbs 51 g, Fibre 5 g

Air Fryer Double Chocolate Muffins

Prep Time: 5 minutes
Cooking Time: 15 minutes
Additional Time: 15 minutes
Total Time: 35 minutes
Servings: 8
Difficulty: Easy

INGREDIENTS

- 1 medium egg
- 75 g Greek yoghourt
- 50 mL semi-skimmed milk
- 75 mL vegetable oil
- ½ tsp vanilla extract
- 75 g caster sugar
- 100 g self-raising flour
- 30 g cocoa powder
- Pinch of salt
- 100 g dark chocolate chips

DIRECTIONS

1. Preheat the air fryer to a temperature of 160 °C/320 °F.
2. Whisk together the egg, yoghurt, milk, oil, and vanilla extract. Add the caster sugar and mix until combined.
3. Sift the flour and cocoa powder in a separate bowl, then add salt and a majority of the chocolate chips.
4. Spoon the batter into the muffin tins or mini cake tins evenly, then sprinkle the remaining chocolate chips on top.
5. Lift the filled tins into the air fryer basket, and bake until well risen, about 12-15 minutes. Allow the muffins to cool for approximately 15 minutes before serving.

Nutrition Information

Calories 186, Fat 7 g, Saturates 4 g, Sugar 16 g, Sodium 0 g, Protein 5 g, Carbs 26 g, Fibre 3 g

Air Fryer Banana Bread

Prep Time: 15 minutes
Cooking Time: 30 minutes
Total Time: 45 minutes
Servings: 6
Difficulty: Easy

INGREDIENTS

- 2 ripe bananas
- 120 g butter, softened
- 100 g caster sugar
- 200 g self-raising flour
- 2 medium eggs, beaten
- 1 tsp baking powder
- 1 tsp ground cinnamon

DIRECTIONS

1. Mix the butter and sugar together until smooth, then slowly add the eggs and mix until well combined.
2. Add the flour, baking powder, and ground cinnamon. Once mixed well, add in the mashed bananas.
3. Gently stir everything together until well combined, then transfer the batter into a greased baking tin.
4. Bake the bread at a temperature of 160 °C/320 °F for 30 minutes. If the bread needs to be cooked longer, only cook it in 5-minute increments to prevent burning.

Nutrition Information

Calories 288, Fat 14 g, Saturates 8 g, Sugar 16 g, Sodium 472 mg, Protein 4 g, Carbs 38 g, Fibre 2 g

Apple Turnover

Prep Time: 10 minutes
Cooking Time: 10 minutes
Total Time: 20 minutes
Servings: 4
Difficulty: Not too tricky

INGREDIENTS

- 2 bramley apples, or 3 if a smaller variety, peeled and diced
- 2 tbsp brown sugar
- 1 tsp ground cinnamon
- 1 tbsp lemon juice
- 320 g puff pastry
- 2 tbsp milk

DIRECTIONS

1. Mix the 2 tbsp brown sugar, ground cinnamon, and lemon juice with the peeled and diced apples in a large bowl until coated.
2. Place the apples in the air fryer and cook for 10 minutes at 190 °C/380 °F, shaking the basket at the halfway mark of cooking.
3. Cut the puff pastry into 4 equal sizes and lay them out on a lightly floured work surface.
4. Divide the cooked apple among the pastry pieces, placing the apples on one side of the pastry and leaving a 1cm gap along the edges.
5. Baste the edges of the puff pastry with milk before folding the pastry over with a pastry brush.
6. Baste the tops of the apple turnovers with milk and poke a hole in the top to allow steam to escape during baking.
7. Transfer the apple turnovers to the air fryer basket, cooking for 10-12 minutes at the same temperature as before. Flip the turnovers halfway through the cooking time. When finished, the puff pastry should be golden brown and flaky.

Nutrition Information

Calories 510, Fat 31 g, Saturates 5 g, Sugar 13g, Sodium 209 mg, Protein 6 g, Carbs 53 g, Fibre 4 g

Air Fryer Apricot and Raisin Cake

Prep Time: 10 minutes
Cooking Time: 12 minutes
Total Time: 22 minutes
Servings: 8
Difficulty: Easy

INGREDIENTS

- 75 g dried apricots
- 4 tbsp orange juice
- 75 g self-raising flour
- 40 g sugar
- 1 egg
- 75 g raisins

DIRECTIONS

1. Preheat the air fryer to 160 °C/320 °F.
2. In a blender, blend the dried apricots and orange juice until smooth.
3. Mix the flour and sugar in a separate bowl together.
4. Beat the egg, then add to the flour-sugar mixture. Add the apricot puree and raisins, then combine all of the ingredients together.
5. Spray an air fryer-safe baking pan with spray oil, then transfer over the cake batter.
6. Cook the cake in the air fryer for 12 minutes, but check on it around the 10-minute mark.
7. Allow the cake to cool off a bit before removing it from the tin and slicing it into it.

Nutrition Information

Calories 116, Fat 1 g, Saturates 0 g,
Sugar 16 g, Sodium 123 mg, Protein 2 g,
Carbs 26 g, Fibre 1 g

Air Fryer Carrot Cake

Prep Time: 10 minutes
Cooking Time: 25 minutes
Total Time: 35 minutes
Servings: 6-8
Difficulty: Not too tricky

INGREDIENTS

- 140 g soft brown sugar
- 2 eggs, beaten
- 140 g butter
- 1 orange, zested and juiced
- 200 g self-raising flour
- 1 tsp ground cinnamon
- 175 g grated carrot
- 60 g sultanas

DIRECTIONS

1. Preheat the air fryer temperature to 175 °C/350 °F.
2. Cream the butter and sugar in a bowl together. Slowly add the beaten eggs, mixing well.
3. Fold in the flour, mixing as you go. Add the orange juice and zest, in addition to the grated carrots and sultanas. Gently mix the ingredients together.
4. Grease a baking tin with a size that will fit in your air fryer and pour the carrot cake batter in.
5. Place the baking tin in the air fryer and bake for 25-30 minutes, checking to see if it is cooked around the 25-minute mark.
6. Allow the cake to cool for approximately 10 minutes before removing it from the cake tin.

Nutrition Information

Calories 191, Fat 1 g, Saturates 1g,
Sugar 28 g, Sodium 176 mg, Protein 3 g,
Carbs 41 g, Fibre 1 g

Air Fryer Chocolate and Chilli Brownies

Prep Time: 10 minutes
Cooking Time: 20 minutes
Total Time: 30 minutes
Servings: 4
Difficulty: Not too tricky

INGREDIENTS

- 200 g butter, melted
- 100 g cocoa powder
- 75 g dark chocolate, melted
- 2 large eggs
- 150 g caster sugar
- ½ tsp vanilla essence
- 150 g self-raising flour
- 1 tbsp crushed dried chilli flakes

DIRECTIONS

1. Preheat the air fryer to a temperature of 180 °C/350 °F.
2. Mix the butter, sugar, and dried chillies together.
3. Beat the eggs, then add them in. Add the melted chocolate and vanilla essence to the mixture following that.
4. Slowly add in the flour and cocoa powder, mixing gently and taking care not to over-stir.
5. Use a greased or parchment paper-lined tin and pour the brownie batter into the tin.
6. Bake the brownies in the air fryer for 15-20 minutes, checking a few times to make sure that the top isn't burning. Add foil to the top if it is cooking too quickly.

Nutrition Information

Calories 385, Fat 18 g, Saturates 11 g, Sugar 38 g, Sodium 181 mg, Protein 6 g, Carbs 54 g, Fibre 3 g

Air Fryer Churros

Prep Time: 10 minutes
Cooking Time: 10 minutes
Additional Time: 1 hour
Total Time: 1 hour 20 minutes
Servings: 8
Difficulty: Show off

INGREDIENTS

- 1 cup water
- 1/3 cup unsalted butter, cut into cubes
- 2 tbsp granulated sugar
- 1 c all-purpose flour
- 2 large eggs
- 1 tsp vanilla extract
- Oil spray

Coating

- ½ c granulated sugar
- ¾ tsp ground cinnamon

DIRECTIONS

1. Add a silicone baking mat to a baking sheet and spray with oil spray.
2. Add the water, butter, sugar, and salt to a saucepan. Bring the solution to a boil on medium-high heat.
3. Reduce the heat to medium-low, then add in the flour, stirring constantly with a rubber spatula. Cook until the dough comes together well and is smooth.
4. Remove the dough from the heat and transfer it to a mixing bowl, and let it cook for 4 minutes.
5. Add eggs and vanilla extract to the dough, then combine. Press the dough into lumps, then transfer it to a large piping bag with a star-shaped tip.
6. Pipe the churros on the baking mat, about 10 cm long. Cut the end with scissors.
7. Let the churros sit in the fridge for 1 hour to set.
8. Transfer the churros to the air fryer and cook for 10-12 minutes at 190 °C/380 °F until the churros are golden brown.
9. In a shallow bowl, combine the granulated sugar and cinnamon coating.
10. Immediately transfer the churros to the bowl to coat them in cinnamon sugar.

Nutrition Information

Calories 204, Fat 9 g, Saturates 5 g, Sugar 15 g, Sodium 91 mg, Protein 3 g, Carbs 27 g

Air Fryer S'mores

Prep Time: 0 minutes
Cooking Time: 4 minutes
Total Time: 4 minutes
Servings: 4
Difficulty: Easy

INGREDIENTS

- 12 Hershey's chocolate squares (1 Hershey's bar)
- 4 marshmallows
- 4 graham cracker sheets, broken in ½

DIRECTIONS

1. Preheat the air fryer temperature setting to 190 °C/380 °F.
2. Place the graham cracker in the air fryer, topping it with a marshmallow. Place a wire or grill rack on top of the marshmallows to prevent them from moving around during cook time.
3. Cook for 3-4 minutes, until golden brown.
4. Remove the s'mores from the air fryer, then top with 3 squares of chocolate and the second half of the graham cracker.

Nutrition Information

Calories 216, Fat 9 g, Saturates 5 g, Sugar 20 g, Sodium 94 mg, Protein 3 g, Carbs 32 g, Fibre 1 g

Air Fryer Bread Pudding

Prep Time: 5 minutes
Cooking Time: 15 minutes
Total Time: 20 minutes
Servings: 2
Difficulty: Not too tricky

INGREDIENTS

- 2 eggs
- 1 c milk
- 3-5 tbsp sugar
- 2 slice toast
- Optional: ice cream, honey, powdered sugar

DIRECTIONS

1. In an oven-safe container, mix the eggs, milk, and 3 tbsp sugar until combined.
2. Rip the toast into 3 cm pieces and add it to the container. Coat the bread in the egg mixture well.
3. Sprinkle sugar on top, approximately 1-2 tbsp.
4. Air fry the bread pudding for 15 minutes at 175 °C/350 °F, until crispy on top.
5. Serve with ice cream, honey, or powdered sugar.

Nutrition Information

Calories 384, Fat 17 g, Saturates 9 g, Sugar 29 g, Sodium 373 mg, Protein 9 g, Carbs 50 g, Fibre 2 g

Air Fried Bananas

Prep Time: 5 minutes
Cooking Time: 6 minutes
Total Time: 11 minutes
Servings: 4
Difficulty: Easy

INGREDIENTS

- 4 yellow bananas
- 2 tsp coconut oil
- ½ tsp - 1 tsp cinnamon
- Coarse pink sea salt

DIRECTIONS

1. Peel each banana and cut the ends off so that it is flat. Then slice into 2 cm pieces.
2. Lay the bananas inside the air fryer basket, then brush the tops with coconut oil. Sprinkle the bananas with ground cinnamon. You may need to divide the bananas into batches so that the bananas cook evenly.
3. Cook the bananas at 180°C/375 °F for 6 minutes.
4. Serve and sprinkle with sea salt.

Nutrition Information

Calories 124, Fat 2 g, Saturates 2 g, Sugar 14 g, Sodium 1 mg, Protein 1 g, Carbs 28 g, Fibre 3 g

Air Fried Oreos

Prep Time: 0 minutes
Cooking Time: 15 minutes
Total Time: 15 minutes
Servings: 12
Difficulty: Easy

INGREDIENTS

- 1 large egg
- ¼ c milk
- 1 tsp vanilla extract
- 1 c pancake and baking mix
- 2 tbsp granulated sugar
- Nonstick cooking spray
- 12 chocolate sandwich cookies (like Oreos)
- Confectioner's sugar for dusting

DIRECTIONS

1. Cut out 2 sheets of parchment paper from the roll to fit the perimeter of the air fryer basket without hanging over.
2. Preheat the air fryer temperature to 175 °C/350 °F.
3. Whisk the eggs, milk, and vanilla into a medium bowl. Add the pancake mix and granulated sugar. The batter should be thick. Add 1 tbsp pancake mix at a time if it seems too thin.
4. Line the air fryer with parchment paper and spray it with cooking spray. Dip 6 of the sandwich cookies into the pancake batter, then let the excess batter drip back into the bowl, then arrange the cookies on the parchment in a single layer. Air fry for 7 minutes until the batter is puffed up and golden.
5. Remove and repeat with the other cookies. Dust the cookies with a sprinkle of powdered sugar before serving.

Nutrition Information

Calories 311, Fat 17 g, Saturates 6 g, Sugar 16 g, Sodium 538 mg, Protein 3 g, Carbs 40 g, Fibre 1 g

Air Fryer Ice Cream Balls

Prep Time: 15 minutes
Cooking Time: 2 minutes
Additional Time: 12 hours
Total Time: 12 hours 17 minutes
Servings: 12
Difficulty: Show off

INGREDIENTS

- 1.5 L good-quality vanilla ice cream
- 300 g plain digestive biscuits, crushed
- 3 eggs
- ½ tbsp milk

DIRECTIONS

1. Place a baking tray in the freezer for 10 minutes.
2. Line the tray with baking paper. Working quickly, scoop the ice cream into 12 evenly-sized balls and place them on the prepared tray. Place them in the freezer for 4 hours, until firm.
3. Place the crushed biscuits in a shallow bowl. One at a time, roll the ice cream balls into the crushed biscuits to coat, shaking off the excess. Return them to the tray and freeze them for another hour.
4. Whisk together the eggs and milk in a bowl. Dip each of the balls into the egg mixture, followed by the crushed biscuits, in order to double-coat. Freeze overnight until very firm.
5. Preheat the air fryer temperature to 200 °C/400 °F.
6. Place 2 ice cream balls on a sheet of parchment paper in the air fryer for 2 minutes at a time. Transfer the balls to a serving plate, and top with your favourite ice cream toppings.

Nutrition Information

Calories 376, Fat 22 g, Saturates 12 g,
Sugar 21 g, Sodium 600 mg, Protein 9 g,
Carbs 36 g, Fibre 2 g

Air Fryer Doughnuts

Prep Time: 30 minutes
Cooking Time: 25 minutes
Additional Time: 2 hours 10 minutes
Total Time: 3 hours 5 minutes
Servings: 6-8
Difficulty: Show off

INGREDIENTS

Doughnut Dough
- 125 mL milk, lukewarm
- 50 g unsalted butter, melted, then cooled to lukewarm
- 7 g package of dried fast-acting yeast
- 60 g caster sugar
- 1 tsp vanilla extract
- 275 g plain flour
- ½ tsp ground cinnamon (optional)
- 1 egg, beaten

Glaze
- 125 g icing sugar
- 3 tbsp milk
- ¼ tsp vanilla extract
- Flavourless oil

DIRECTIONS

1. Combine the milk, melted butter, yeast, 1 tsp caster sugar, and vanilla extract into a bowl. Leave the mixture for 10 minutes for the yeast to activate.
2. In a separate bowl, measure out the remaining sugar, flour, ½ tsp salt, and cinnamon (optional). Mix the egg into the milk mixture, followed by the dry ingredients.
3. Knead the dough with a hook attachment in your standing mixer on medium speed for 5-8 minutes. You want the dough to be smooth and elastic. If you do not have a standing mixer in your kitchen, you can knead the dough for 10-12 minutes by hand until it is smooth. Expect a very sticky dough.
4. Transfer the dough to a lightly-oiled bowl, and cover with a clean tea towel for 1 hour 30 minutes, until the dough has doubled in size. Tip the dough out onto a lightly floured work surface, and roll out the dough until it is about 1.5 cm thick.
5. Cut the doughnuts using a doughnut cutter or two circular cutters of different sizes.
6. Place the doughnuts well-spaced on a lined baking sheet and cover the baking sheet with a clean tea towel. Leave the doughnuts to rise for 40 minutes or overnight in the fridge.
7. When you are ready to cook, place 2-3 doughnuts in the air fryer basket and cook them at 180 °C/360 °F for 5-6 minutes or until golden in colour. If you are worried about the doughnuts sticking, you can add a layer of parchment baking paper to the air fryer basket.
8. As they finish cooking, remove the doughnuts from the basket and leave them to cool on a wire rack.
9. While the final batch is cooking, sift the icing sugar into a bowl, and add the milk and vanilla extract. When the doughnuts have cooled, dip the tops of each one in the glaze and leave them on the wire rack to set.

Nutrition Information

Calories 290, Fat 7 g, Saturates 4 g,
Sugar 24 g, Sodium 0 g, Protein 6 g,
Carbs 51 g, Fibre 1 g

CONCLUSION

Cooking can be one's happy place. Where the stresses of the daily grind melt away, where creativity roams, and where both hunger and taste experience simultaneous satisfaction. We hope that this resource has equipped you to take on the mysteries of entering your own kitchen with confidence and unlocking a new potential to cook exotic or classical British meals with the comfort and ease of one kitchen tool - the air fryer.

We have shown you everything from cooking meals for sunrise breakfasts to sundown desserts and everything in-between. Daily meal preparation and execution has never been easier than the present, and our 150-recipe resource bank makes no excuse for even the busiest of people to slow down and make a quick, healthy meal to fuel their busy lives.

The kitchen isn't as foreign anymore. With simple ingredients and simple recipes, you are now more able than ever before to provide the nutritious, easy, and delicious meals that your family needs to connect over dinner table discussions and dreamy over dreamy desserts.

Get your apron on and get cooking - there's a world of recipes at your fingertips!